BUILD STRONG

FINISH FIRST IN LIFE, LOVE, AND WORK

By Steve Vaggalis

destinyworshipcenter.com

BUILD STRONG: Finish First in Life, Love, and Work

Hardcover: ISBN 978-0-578-41983-1

Paperback: ISBN 978-0-578-44024-8

Editor: Linda A. Schantz
Cover Design: Josh Kidd, Jessica Preskitt

As my first book,
I want to dedicate this work
to my church family
at Destiny Worship Center.
You have loved me
and inspired me to
Build Strong.

CONTENTS

A WORD FROM
THE AUTHOR

I'm proud of my Greek heritage—the food, the language, the passion for friends and family, the food. (Did I already mention the food?) My dad was born in Greece, and I grew up speaking both English and Greek at home. Dad, who was a pastor, would even have me translate his sermons into Greek. It was difficult work, but I appreciate the experience now.

When you think of Greece and Greek culture, I'm guessing a few things come to mind immediately:

» The food (of course), followed by smashing plates (sometimes).

» The Olympics (The games got their start on the ancient plains of Olympus, Greece, more than seven hundred years before Christ was born.)

» The architecture (especially the Parthenon—one of the most famous structures in the world, which was built twenty-five centuries ago with its great Doric columns—much of which is still standing to this day).

It's fitting to think momentarily about classic Greek architecture and the history of the great Olympic contests as we begin this book.

Just as balance and proportion are hallmarks of the ancient marble-columned buildings in the country of my ancestors, I believe there are seven key principles that work together as girders and scaffolds—PILLARS, if you will—to help us build and support a strong Christian life. These seven pillars not only hold up and reinforce the structure of our lives and households, but they also serve as mighty bulwarks to help us stay standing through the storms and uncertainty of today's troubled times.

Friends, as you read through these pages, it is my desire that you will be guided by the Great Master Builder's hand. I pray that these lessons will give you the hammers and chisels you need to craft your life and your home into a mighty tower of God's strength and purpose. And, no matter what storms may come to try to knock you off course, as you take the steps to build your life on a firm foundation, I believe you'll finish your race with your eye on the prize of the high calling of Christ Jesus.

May God's blessing be yours on the journey,

Pastor Steve Vaggalis

INTRODUCTION

I just don't measure up.

I'm not where I thought I'd be at this point in life.

Why doesn't anything ever come easy for me?

Do these thoughts ever cross your mind? Perhaps, some days, they dominate your thoughts.

Don't worry, my friend. If you've had these thoughts, you're not alone.

So many people are missing out on the abundant life Jesus Christ has for them. They know life should be different. They know it should be better—but how?

These feelings of inadequacy are real. All I have to do is look in a mirror or see pictures of my younger self to be reminded.

Growing up, I was always in the shadow of my brother. Pete is seventeen months older than me. He's the stereotypical firstborn overachiever. When we were growing up, he excelled in everything, from the classroom to sports. Teachers and coaches loved him. He had lots of friends. In fact, I'd hang out around him a lot just hoping to steal a few. Big brother Pete got me back for that, though. In third grade he stole my first girlfriend!

A few years later Pete became the talk of Ontario Middle School in Mansfield, Ohio, when he made a half-court basketball shot at the buzzer to win a game. The crowd carried him off the court on their shoulders, parading him around the gym. Later, when we moved away, thirty or forty friends came by to say goodbye and bring him gifts.

As I got older, I felt completely overshadowed. Pete was always the class hero. He was the popular one. Pete was the portrait. I was the silhouette.

As a kid, I hid my feelings the best way I could. I was never outwardly competitive with Pete, and through it all, we actually had a close relationship. One day Pete saw a kid picking on me in front of our house. My dad was a pastor, and the parsonage where we lived was right next to the church. Pete knew I didn't have what it took to take on that bully, so right there, in the church parking lot, Pete pushed me aside and fought the kid for me. I was grateful for my deliverance, but that incident was yet another reason I had found to idolize Pete. I thought he hung the moon. I tried to imitate him. Still, there was no way I could measure up.

I've struggled with this sense of inferiority all my life, in various situations and with various people. The feelings of being inadequate—being *less than*—plague us all.

SECOND BORN, SECOND RATE?

Things finally started to turn my way when I found Christ. I read the Bible more closely, wanting to model my life after history's men of God. I was amazed to discover that a great many Bible heroes had every reason to feel inferior, but still, they lived lives that found them favor with the Lord.

The textbook example of this is David, in the Old Testament. What would you think if you were told to stay in the fields, tending sheep, while each one of your eleven older brothers were paraded before Samuel as candidates to become the next king? Yet a few years later, David, the red-headed shepherd boy found himself in the middle of God's blessing and favor in the palace as the ruler of the nation.

In the New Testament, the Apostle Paul declared, "I am the least of the apostles and do not even deserve to be called an apostle, because I persecuted the church of God" (1 Corinthians 15:9 NIV). Talk about some feelings of inferiority! Yet after Paul met the Lord on that Damascus Road, he could have coasted quietly in this race we call life. But, no, the Bible says Paul strived to "run in such a way as to get the prize" (1 Corinthians 9:24 NIV).

And here's the beauty of seeking the prize of God's blessing: **Just because you finish first, that doesn't mean someone else has to finish**

second! God's Word makes it clear that we're not competing against each other.

Perhaps one of the most misunderstood people in the Bible, and someone born under a huge shadow of inferiority, was Jacob. It is his story we will be focusing on in our studies throughout this book.

The son of Isaac, Jacob was born second to his twin brother, Esau. Jacob is known by most readers of Scripture as "the deceiver," the one who cheated Esau out of his birthright. And while that is one Hebrew meaning of his name, Jacob deserves to be seen in a different light than what is typically taught in Sunday school.

Despite what you might have been told, Jacob had the right priorities. He wasn't perfect, but he did exemplify the pursuit of God's plan for his life. And, oh, how he was rewarded!

Even though Jacob was born second, he would become the third and final patriarch of Israel. When God spoke to Moses in the burning bush, He said, "I am the God of your father, the God of Abraham, the God of Isaac, and the God of Jacob" (Exodus 3:6 NIV). God didn't say, "I am the God of Abraham, the God of Isaac, and the God of that no-good, cheater Jacob." The Lord of second chances used the man whom many might see as inferior to build His people and to build His family.

Jacob was born second, but he finished first.

To be clear, when I write about being *second* in these studies, I'm referring to that sense of not measuring up. This feeling can hit anyone—the firstborn, second born, fourth born, eighth born, at any time in life—especially when we start comparing ourselves to others. Usually all it takes for us to feel second rate is being around someone who appears to be more gifted, smarter, or more successful than we are—or it could even be someone with a bigger small group than we have at church!

The feelings of being *less than* can come at any time, and just because you've conquered them once, that doesn't mean they won't come at you again from time to time. I'm sure there were many times when even great Bible heroes like Jacob, David, and Paul had to fight back the negative feelings and lean in to walk in the victory God had for them.

For me, it was years after college when I experienced another season of feeling second born that was similar to the feelings I'd had around my brother Pete. After being on staff at a church for fourteen years, my pastor encouraged me to plant a church in Destin, Florida. I felt so overwhelmed.

Who am I to start a church? I thought. And to top it off, I didn't even really know how to go about it. These days, there are a number of great church-planting networks, with wonderful resources and training, but back then, few, if any, healthy models existed. So, as inadequate for the job as I felt, I knew I had to look to God for His wisdom to build a strong church.

Not surprisingly, along the way, I've discovered that it's His wisdom which has made all the difference for me. From how to find a godly wife to how to raise a strong family to how to lead a large organization, wisdom has been the key to unlocking the doors to God's blessing and success in my life.

Along the journey, I've discovered seven key principles from the story of Jacob that are also woven throughout the Bible to help you build a strong and overcoming life in Christ.

In this study, I want to explore each of these seven pillars with you. I've set them up as an acronym, so they're easy to commit to memory.

P R I O R I T I E S

I N T E G R I T Y

L O Y A L T Y

L O V E

A C C O U N T A B I L I T Y

R I G H T E O U S N E S S

S T E W A R D S H I P

I believe these seven things are the "finish first" essentials I need in my life and you need in yours. It's my prayer that you will see ways you can put them into practice for yourself, for your family, for your career, and for God's kingdom.

I truly believe feelings of inferiority can only be banished with God's wisdom and grace. Receiving an unexpected compliment, a promotion at work, an A in a class—these and other 'victories' feel good—but I know from experience, the high doesn't last long.

If you are not pursuing success God's way, it won't be long before you again feel second rate. It's not what you have; it's *Who you have* that makes the difference.

Before you turn the page and begin your study, the absolute good news I want to cement in your heart and mind is that *you can build a strong life*.

You can finish first in life, love, and work.

And as the famous Chinese proverb says, "The journey of a thousand miles begins with a single step."

The first step is to lay the foundation of God's wisdom in your life to see where He wants you to go.

LAYING THE FOUNDATION

WISDOM TO BUILD A STRONG HOUSE

Wisdom has built her house. She has hewn out her seven pillars.

Proverbs 9:1 NKJV

Most people equate the word wisdom with knowledge. Some take it a step further and say wisdom is actually the application of knowledge. Still others think wisdom is simply a function of experience or age.

But age doesn't guarantee wisdom, does it? We all know people in their thirties and forties who are struggling today because of their choices in life. And there are twenty-year-olds to whom people say, "You are wise beyond your years."

Wisdom is not the same as experience. I once heard someone say, "Experience is what you use to recognize all the mistakes you've repeated." Isn't that the truth?!

So, if wisdom isn't knowledge or the application of knowledge or even experience, what is it?

What does the Bible say wisdom is?

The word *wisdom* in the Greek is the word *"sofia."* When translated, this word literally means skill. So then wisdom isn't just knowledge. It's a skill. But it's not just any kind of skill.

In the book of James, we read:

If any of you lacks wisdom, let him ask of God, who gives to all liberally and without reproach, and it will be given to him.

James 1:5 NKJV

So, then, wisdom is not a human gift. No, it's something special. James writes that wisdom is a *God-given* skill.

But what is that skill?!

Wisdom is the principal thing; therefore get wisdom.

Proverbs 4:7 NKJV

The Hebrew word translated *principal* in that verse doesn't just mean that wisdom is the most important thing, although it is. That word is also translated as *preeminent*—or more literally, as it's rendered in many versions of the Bible—as *the beginning*.

What can we gather from this about the skill of wisdom?

Wisdom is the God-given skill to see the reaping before the sowing.

It's the God-given ability to see the **end** of a thing *before* its **beginning**.

STEP OUT OF TODAY AND INTO THE FUTURE

Have you ever made a decision in life that you regret? If you could have seen then what you know now, you know you wouldn't have made that choice.

Maybe you're weighed down by regrets. By thoughts of, *Oh, if only I hadn't...* or *If only I had...* or *Maybe I shouldn't have....* If you're carrying around thoughts of regret, trust me, you're not alone.

One of my biggest regrets in life is losing a great friend—all over a silly tuxedo. There was a time when things were tough for me. They were so tough I was living out of my car. But a good friend took me in and gave me a place to stay. He owned a men's clothing store and was extremely generous to me. But a few years later, when it was time for my wedding, I wanted a particular style of tuxedo and went to a different store. I lacked the wisdom to realize my decision would hurt him. I wasn't thinking of him and our future friendship. All I wanted was that silly tuxedo. And for that I paid a steep price. It cost me a dear friend.

Now, there are two things we can do with our regrets: We can beat ourselves up about them over and over, or we can learn from them and determine to pursue the wisdom that will help us to foresee and avoid future missteps.

Wisdom enables us to step out of today and look into the future. It allows us to envision the consequences of our decisions before we act on them—decisions that would affect us and those we love.

> *Wisdom is the God-given skill to see the reaping before the sowing.*

Wisdom allows us to be able to see the results of what we're sowing ahead of time. It allows us to look into the future and see what's going to happen. Then wisdom brings us back to today, and asks, "Did you like what you saw?"

If you don't like the harvest, don't sow the seed.

Wisdom is the skill of being able to see the future through God's eyes.

LAYING THE FOUNDATION OF WISDOM

The Bible connects wisdom and foresight, most notably with how to build a life and a home.

One of our key scriptures for this book, Proverbs 9:1 says, "Wisdom has built her house; She has hewn out her seven pillars" (NKJV). But before any pillars can be erected, and before any walls can be built, the proper foundation must be laid.

The foundation is wisdom.

Jesus Himself said:

> *Everyone who hears these words of mine and puts them into practice is like a wise man who built his house on the rock. The rain came down, the streams rose, and the winds blew and beat against that house; yet it did not fall, because it had its foundation on the rock. But everyone who hears these words of mine and does not put them into practice is like a foolish man who built his house*

on sand. The rain came down, the streams rose, and the winds blew and beat against that house, and it fell with a great crash.

Matthew 7:24–27 NIV

In 1 Corinthians 3:10, Paul says, "According to the grace of God which was given to me, as a *wise master builder* I have laid the foundation…" The Greek word translated as *master builder* is *"architekton."* Obviously this is where we get our word, "architect."

Paul said he was building his life like a wise architect. An architect creates a finished building on paper, long before any construction begins. In this verse, Paul was explaining to the church at Corinth that he could envision what he wanted to build in them, what he wanted to accomplish for the Lord. Paul could see God's plan in his mind's eye, because God had given him the skill of wisdom. He could see the future God had planned.

What is it that you see? Do you have a picture of what God wants for you? If you have a family, I know with certainty God wants you to be the architect of your own home. He wants you to be a wise and skilled craftsman. We are to be wise builders of our lives and the lives of those we have influence over.

What do you see? Do you have a picture of what God wants for you?

God wants to show you how to build your life, the life of your spouse, and the lives of your children. Get a picture of what God wants for you and how your life should be. God wants you to see the blueprints of your future home through His eyes.

Lord, show me how to have a healthy, strong, vibrant, life-giving home with You at the center of it, so that when the storms come and the winds blow, nothing will be destroyed or depleted, in Jesus' name. Amen.

This is a life-giving prayer and one that isn't to be prayed just once. I encourage you to pray this on a weekly and even daily basis, especially when you are going through your own *second-born season*. It's vitally important to keep this in focus, because we know the storms will come. It's not a matter of if—but when.

If you feel as if you're inadequate, and life has gotten you down, take heart in knowing that God wants to give you His wisdom.

WISDOM HAS AN EVIL TWIN

As we are seeking wisdom to build our lives, we need to be on guard. There are two kinds of wisdom in this world. And just as Jacob had a twin who didn't care about the things of God, godly wisdom has an evil twin.

The Bible warns us about an evil wisdom that "does not descend from above, but is earthly, sensual, demonic" (James 3:15 NKJV). The King James Version of the Scriptures says it's "devilish." It downplays the consequences of our impending actions and focuses on our feelings instead. But feelings lie, just as the serpent lied to Eve. Worldly wisdom tells us, "Nothing is going to happen. No, nothing at all. Go ahead and do what you feel."

There will always be a battle between the world's way and God's wisdom, and you must be able to discern between the two.

There is a simple way you can tell the difference. God's wisdom is not just advice. God doesn't simply give us suggestions. His wisdom is strong. It says, "This is what is going to happen if you make these choices." God's wisdom is based on the future.

Esau, Jacob's twin brother, was a picture of this worldly type of wisdom. Jacob was a picture of the heavenly. Again, Jacob wasn't perfect, but Esau made the mistake of his life. Esau came in one day, hot and hungry from hunting, and he couldn't see the end result of his immediate choices. He couldn't see the value of the double portion that was his rightful birthright as the first born, and Esau sold his birthright to Jacob for a bowl of soup!

Worldly wisdom will make you surrender something valuable for something that's fleeting.

Just like Jacob and Esau wrestled inside their mother's womb, this battle of earthly and heavenly wisdom has been raging within mankind all the way back to the Garden of Eden. God said to Adam and Eve, "The day you eat of the tree, you will surely die."

Think about it for a second. That was hardly a warm interaction or friendly advice. But it shows us how God's wisdom operates and what a caring and good Father He is. Not only does God tell His children what to do and what not to do, He even tells us what will happen as the end result.

He is completely transparent and will never hide the truth from us. We can trust Him completely.

That snake, the devil, on the other hand, always challenges us to doubt what God has said.

> *… And he [the serpent] said to the woman, "Has God indeed said, 'You shall not eat of every tree of the garden'?"*
>
> *And the woman said to the serpent, "We may eat the fruit of the trees of the garden; but of the fruit of the tree which is in the midst of the garden, God has said, 'You shall not eat it, nor shall you touch it, lest you die.'"*
>
> *Then the serpent said to the woman, "You will not surely die. For God knows that in the day you eat of it your eyes will be opened, and you will be like God, knowing good and evil."*
>
> *Genesis 3:1–5 NKJV*

Maybe Eve was feeling a little bit of inferiority, wanting to be like God. I don't know, but whatever the reason, Eve couldn't resist. Adam and Eve ate the fruit and fell for the lie the devil was peddling.

The enemy always paints the wrong picture. He paints an evil picture that diverts our attention from God and keeps us from finishing first. If we fall into his trap, we'll always end up with regrets.

God's heart for us is to make the right choices. His wisdom will show us the outcomes before we act. We don't have to accept the world's wisdom and advice. **If we can see ahead to the outcomes we want to happen, we can back up to make the choices that will bring the desired endings to pass.**

Wisdom's evil twin wants us to make choices that give us good feelings in the moment, but the ending always brings us death and destruction.

The wisdom from above knows when to say "No, not now," instead of "What was I thinking, and how?"

WISDOM IS THE EQUALIZER

I know life isn't automatically rosy for firstborns. In Bible times, firstborns had remarkable privileges. These days, life can be challenging for all of us, no matter if we were born first, third, or seventh in our families. I do believe, however, that God has a special place in His heart for underdogs—for those who feel *second* in life. God anointed Abraham's second son, Isaac, and it was Isaac's second son, Jacob, whom God blessed. Even Jesus is called the second Adam in 1 Corinthians 15.

And Solomon was a second born, too. Many people regard Solomon as Israel's greatest king, but early on, he was well aware of his shortcomings. The second-born son of David and Bathsheba, Solomon, took the reign from his father and humbly approached God to help him lead the nation:

> *Solomon went up to the bronze altar before the Lord in the tent of meeting and offered a thousand burnt offerings on it. That night God appeared to Solomon, and said to him, "Ask for whatever you want me to give you."*

God's wisdom will show you how to defeat sin and walk in victory.

> *Solomon answered God, "You have shown great kindness to David my father and have made me king in his place.... Give me wisdom and knowledge that I may lead this people, for who is able to govern this great people of yours?"*
>
> 1 Chronicles 1:6–10 NIV

Smart king, that Solomon. In Proverbs 3:5–6, he records for our sake, "Trust in the Lord with all your heart, and lean not on your own understanding; in all your ways acknowledge Him, and He shall direct your paths" (NKJV). But the secret that made Solomon so great is actually found in verse 7: *"Do not be wise in your own eyes...."*

Solomon sought wisdom from the Lord, and because of that, God promised to grant the earthly king riches, honor, length of days, and victory (1 Chronicles 1:11–12).

Wisdom is the principal thing. The ability to prosper comes with wisdom. The ability to learn what to do comes with wisdom. With wisdom, you have the ability to learn how to take care of your body so you can have length of days. God's wisdom will show you how to defeat sin and walk in victory. The secret is to ask Him for wisdom. God wants to bring wisdom into your life so you can excel in ways you've never known before.

Today you may feel overwhelmed by real or imagined limitations and shortcomings. You may question whether you have the ability to accomplish certain things in your life. Let me tell you: **Wisdom is your equalizer.**

You may be wondering, "How do I recover from this last financial downturn?" It won't happen through your own skill. It will come through God's skill—wisdom. "How do I win back my wife and family? My ways have driven them away." Ask God to give you wisdom. He'll help you to bring them back, and He'll also show you what you were doing wrong that pushed them away. Seek the Lord's wisdom and let it bring you what you're lacking.

> *Lord, equalize my limitations and inferiorities, and make the difference in my life. Where I am weak, make me strong. What I lack, You can provide. Lord give me wisdom, in Jesus' name. Amen.*

WISDOM COMES FROM AN ENCOUNTER WITH GOD

> *Then he [Jacob] dreamed, and behold, a ladder was set up on the earth, and its top reached to heaven; and there the angels of God were ascending and descending on it.*
>
> *Genesis 28:12 NKJV*

Like Solomon, Jacob was a man of God who needed God's wisdom to succeed and to lead His people. Jacob's dream involved a ladder set on the Earth. The top reached all the way to Heaven and angels ascended and descended upon it. This dream was God's message to Jacob that he would build his family with access to heavenly wisdom.

It's as if God was saying to him, "Jacob, you can't build this nation with your limitations, but I'm giving you a picture to show you that your earthly challenges can be met with heavenly solutions. If you'll bring your problems and concerns up to Me, I'll touch them and give you My wisdom for the answers."

Jacob was the second-born. He was broke and running away from his brother Esau. He didn't have the blessings of the birthright yet, but because he looked to God for wisdom, God blessed him far above the wisdom of the world.

God blessed Jacob and made him rich. He made him the father of a nation. He blessed him beyond belief. The wisdom of God far exceeds the wisdom of this world. The wisdom of men is foolishness to God.

When Jacob woke up from that dream, he said, "This is the house of God, the gate of Heaven!" And in Genesis 28:17, Jacob declared, "How awesome is this place!"

Jacob's enthusiasm makes me wonder, how often do we respond to God like this?

Do we actually realize that God is the source of all wisdom, the source of all sound decision-making? He's the beginning.

> *The fear of the Lord is the beginning of wisdom.*
>
> *Proverbs 9:10 NKJV*

God knows how your decisions will end up ahead of time. He knows the choices you should make in life. And if you seek His wisdom, He will give you His plans for how you should proceed. He will give you His wisdom out of His great love for you.

The key point is this: Wisdom is the ability to see with God's eyes. God doesn't see on a timeline from the *beginning* of something to the *end*. He sees everything from the *end* to the *beginning*.

When God created the world, He didn't blindly proceed from Day One's actions to Day Six, although it's recorded that way. He saw the whole thing in advance! God saw the future for you and me, and said, "They're going to need oxygen to breathe. They're going to need water to bathe in. They're going to need food to eat." God saw the reaping before the sowing, so when humans entered the picture, everything was already in action.

So, how do we lay the foundation of our lives? We lay it with God's wisdom.

Be in awe of Him. Realize He knows the end from the beginning. He wants to show you what He has planned for you, if you'll only come to Him and ask.

God doesn't want you to miss out. You simply need to ask, and His wisdom is yours. **Wisdom is the foundation you need to uphold the seven godly pillars and make your life and your home strong.**

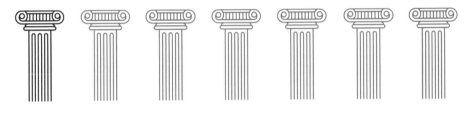

PILLAR 1
PRIORITIES

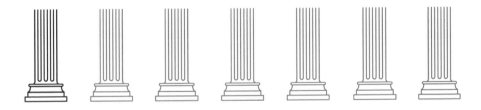

THE PRIORITY OF PRIORITIES

One of my favorite TV programs is *Antiques Roadshow*. Have you seen it? Experts travel from city to city, appraising antiques and collectibles that people bring to the show. The appraisers (all seeming geniuses, in my estimation) always ask how the owner came to possess the item, and then they take time to share their expertise. They talk about who might have produced the artifact, its age, why the piece is particularly special or not—you get the idea.

All that background information is interesting, but it also makes for sheer agony for us viewers and surely for the owners. *Just tell us how much it's worth!* We all want to shout at the TV screen.

I don't recall all the details, but I was watching *Antiques Roadshow* one day, when a guy brought in some sort of American-West-themed sculpture he had picked up at a garage sale. As the appraiser talked up its fine workmanship, you could see the owner get more and more eager for the big reveal. Turns out, according to the expert, that the sculpture would likely fetch up to $35,000 at an auction. Wow!

But as soon as that appraiser got to the point and told the owner how much the sculpture was worth, I wasn't thinking about the guy who just got this amazing news about his art piece anymore. My first thought? *Who sold that thing at a garage sale for $10?!* The poor guy who sold it didn't realize its value or understand the cost of his decision.

We can all have a good laugh about that and think, *Wow, I'm glad that wasn't my garage sale.* But wouldn't it be great if we each had our own personal appraiser? Not to calculate the worth of our possessions—but for something much more import than that. Wouldn't it be amazing if there were someone who could tell us if the choices that present themselves to us in life are valuable and worth pursuing?

Of course, the whole of the Bible serves that purpose:

> *All Scripture is given by inspiration of God, and is profitable for doctrine, for reproof, for correction, for instruction in righteousness, that the man of God may be complete, thoroughly equipped for every good work.*
>
> *2 Timothy 3:16–17 NKJV*

But as we look to the living Word for wisdom, we must never forget that the Author Himself is a living and active God who is always assessing the condition of our hearts:

> *For the eyes of the Lord range throughout the earth to strengthen those whose hearts are fully committed to him….*
>
> *2 Chronicles 16:9 NIV*

In other words, God is looking to make sure we share His priorities so He can strengthen and bless us.

God doesn't examine our outward appearances. As 2 Chronicles makes clear, God is concerned about our hearts. He wants to know who shares His priorities. He wants to bless you and me. He wants to strengthen our hearts for the challenges He knows that lie ahead.

I love this promise in the Psalms:

> *…No good thing will He withhold from those who walk uprightly.*
>
> *Psalm 84:11 NKJV*

God is not looking at you or picking you out of the crowd in order to punish you. We are told God is seeking hearts that are "fully committed to Him." There are consequences if we don't "walk uprightly" and share God's priorities. We must focus on what our God views as important, so we don't put ourselves at risk of bad decisions and jeopardize our futures.

I'm so thankful we have a God who cares about our outcomes. God gives us wisdom when we seek Him and make what He values our highest priority.

The priority of where you place your heart goes back to biblical times, where we once again pick up the story of our man Jacob. Let's take a closer look at his struggle with Esau.

A BATTLE IN THE WOMB

The conflict between Esau and Jacob can be traced back to the rather unusual circumstances of their birth. Midway in the book of Genesis we are told that Isaac was forty years old when he married Rebekah. When the couple couldn't get pregnant, Isaac pleaded with the Lord, and his prayers were answered. The pregnancy was not easy, however, and Rebekah sought the Lord's view of the situation:

> *And the Lord said to her: "Two nations are in your womb, Two peoples shall be separated from your body; One people shall be stronger than the other, And the older shall serve the younger."*
>
> *Genesis 25:23 NKJV*

During birth, Esau was the first to arrive. Jacob followed right behind. Jacob was so close to the front that he grabbed his brother's Esau's heel as they came out. In fact, the Hebrew word for "heel" sounds very similar to the name Jacob.

Being the firstborn son in biblical times was a big deal, much more so than it is today. As the firstborn, Esau had the birthright which gave him a double portion of the family estate and authority over all the family members. Jacob

God gives us wisdom when we make what He values our highest priority.

and Esau were in their mother's womb seemingly fighting over who would be born first and who would receive the blessings of the birthright as a result.

Growing up, the boys' contrasting futures were evident in their personalities and interests. The Bible tells us Esau grew up to become a skilled hunter, "a man of the field." Jacob was described as "a mild man, dwelling in tents" (Genesis 25:27). To put it in modem terms, if you took both men to a mall, Esau would make a beeline to the Bass Pro Shop. Jacob? He'd head to Bed, Bath & Beyond. (Not that there's anything wrong with that.) Jacob just wasn't an outdoorsman like his brother, and this might have cost him the love of his father.

WHEN YOU FEEL UNLOVED

As a kid, I knew my parents loved me, but I have to admit there were times I felt they loved my older brother more. As I said earlier, Pete excelled in most everything he tried. And it was hard to miss all the praise and attention he received. He also had more privileges and freedoms than me. Now I know it's natural for the oldest child to get certain privileges, simply because of his or her age, but back then, as the little brother, I didn't understand that. I equated those privileges to favor. (Nine-year-old me thought, *Pete gets to stay up until 10 P.M. Mom and Dad must love him more!*)

> *God isn't keeping track of whatever earthly thing you're measuring your worth by.*

Fast forwarding to my own parenting adventure, you should have seen my wife and me when we our first-born son came along. There had never been a more baby-proofed home than ours! Jackie and I plugged every single electrical socket, padded every sharp corner in the house, and double-washed every utensil. Even for all our extra care, though, one night we accidentally gave our weeks-old son, Steven, something close to one tablespoon of Benadryl when he was sick, instead of the recommended one-eighth teaspoon. When I realized we had severely miscalculated the dose, I called the ER, panicked.

The doctor's response to this new dad? "Oh, it'll just make him sleep like a baby."

Thanks a lot, Doc!

If you're a mom or dad, you've probably discovered this, but parenting is quite a bit different for the next kid in line. With Victor, our youngest, we practically let him play with bleach! (just kidding) And we joke that it wasn't until his senior year in high school that he finally got a photo or two in the family album!

No matter what stage we're at in life, we all want to know we're special—that we are loved. The feelings of inferiority creep in when we feel as if someone else is getting first billing above us in some way. There are plenty of times we've received the second-highest award or second-best ranking, and, instead of celebrating, we wonder how close the margins were between us and the person who came in first.

Rest assured, God isn't keeping track of your ranking or whatever earthly thing it is you're measuring your worth by. God doesn't look at a rank or a birth order; He looks at the heart and what you do with what He's given you.

Even if you weren't born to receive the inheritance of the family or to win all the awards, you're loved and will receive an eternal inheritance from your Heavenly Father that far outweighs any inheritance or favor you could receive today.

A TROUBLING VERSE

> *...The same Lord is Lord of all and richly blesses all who call on him.*
>
> *Romans 10:12 NIV*

And

> *...Of a truth I perceive that God is no respecter of persons.*
>
> *Acts 10:34 KJV*

Or I like the way The Message Bible puts it:

> *...It's God's own truth, nothing could be plainer: God plays no favorites! It makes no difference who you are or where you're from...*
>
> *Acts 10:34 MSG*

Still, it used to make me wonder, why would Romans 9:13 say, "Jacob have I loved, but Esau have I hated"? It's because of this key thought: **God's favor comes because of right priorities.**

When God knows you have the right priorities in life—when you put what He has done and what He values first—the favor of God comes upon you.

When my wife knows I cherish her and I won't put anyone before her, her favor comes on me and our marriage. She loves me and treasures me, because she knows I put her above all others.

When Esau didn't prioritize and favor what God had brought into his life, it hurt his relationship with God.

God says, I'm rich toward all, but My favor is on those whose priorities are in receiving what I have for them. My eye is on those who favor Me.

God isn't a respecter of persons, but He is a respecter of priorities. Esau did not value what God valued.

PRIORITIES DEFINE OUR VALUES

> But Jacob said, "Sell me your birthright as of this day."
>
> And Esau said, "Look, I am about to die; so what is this birthright to me?"
>
> Then Jacob said, "Swear to me as of this day."
>
> So he swore to him, and sold his birthright to Jacob. And Jacob gave Esau bread and stew of lentils; then he ate and drank, arose, and went his way. Thus Esau despised his birthright.
>
> Genesis 25:31–34 NKJV

God isn't a respecter of persons, but He is a respecter of priorities.

Esau didn't see the value of what God had brought into his life. In fact, **he despised it**.

Our priorities show us what is valuable to our hearts. When Esau despised his birthright and all the favor and promises of God that would have come with it, he made it *worth-less*. It wasn't without worth, but Esau devalued it and accounted the worth of God's favor as less than the value of a bowl of soup.

When we understand what Jesus did for us at the cross, the price He paid for our redemption, and every good and perfect gift God has given to us in life, we will see those things as valuable and precious. We should recognize the great worth God has given us.

Lord, as for me and my house, what You did for us is priceless, and You will always be first place in our home. Help us to make Your priorities our priorities.

The enemy tries to get us to see something in the natural as worth more than something that is spiritual. How often do we exchange something of great spiritual worth for mere trinkets we can see, touch, or feel?

The enemy tricks us into giving up our God-promised blessings and hurting ourselves and our families in the process.

GODLY PRIORITIES PROTECT OUR RELATIONSHIPS

We need to value and protect what God has given us: our spouses, our children, our churches, and our leaders.

In the practice of property law, the word *priority* can be used to describe the rights to a parcel of land. In a legal connotation, a priority is a *claim* or a *boundary*.

In the Vaggalis family, one of my relatives has the title to a piece of property located in Greece. On that document, which is the size of a giant map, the words, "PRIORITY OF CLAIM" are written in big capital letters across the top. This document defines the survey lines and the borders of the land which was deeded to the family. This document defines the boundaries of what belongs to us.

But property isn't the only place where we need to have clearly established boundaries. People will trespass against your boundaries every day and try to change your priorities if you let them. It's setting our priorities—placing value and boundaries around what's important—that protects us and our relationships with those we love.

You can't allow the unimportant to knock down your walls of protection. You have to say, "No, these are my boundaries, and I'm not going to let people trespass against my life or my family and get things out of whack."

When Esau despised the birthright, he put his stomach over the boundaries God had put in place to protect his family. Esau refused to draw the line and guard what God would have given him. In refusing the right to prioritize his family, Esau turned his back on an entire nation.

All for a lousy bowl of soup.

PRIORITIES ARE CHALLENGED BY PRESSING NEEDS

A blessed future hung in the balance for Jacob and Esau. The day Esau came home exhausted and hungry, his appetite deepened the moment he smelled the lentils Jacob had prepared.

And just like that, Esau traded away the most valuable thing he had. Jacob did not deceive him. Esau simply didn't value the things God had promised his family. If Esau were alive today, he would have been the man who sold that rare sculpture in a garage sale for a whopping $10!

And do you know what? It appears Esau was pretty pleased with his soup-for-birthright decision at the time. At least there's no immediate indication that he realized its long-term cost. His pressing need—filling his growling stomach—was satisfied:

> *And Jacob gave Esau bread and stew of lentils; then he ate and drank, arose, and went his way....*
>
> *Genesis 25:34 NKJV*

Pressing needs still get so many people, including good Christians, off track. It happens to all of us sometimes.

You want to make your time with God a priority, but have you ever gone to pray, and then a thousand pressing needs begin to flood your mind?

What are we going to have for breakfast?

Did the kids feed the dog?

Who is posting pictures on Instagram right now?

What color shirt should I wear today?

Esau's hunger was a pressing need. His birthright was a priority. He yielded to the pressing need instead of the priority.

You have to have wisdom—the God-given skill—to be able to discern a true priority from a pressing need. Otherwise people will dictate to you what *your priorities* should be because of *their pressing needs.*

So how do you tell the difference?

A pressing need is about the "now." Your flesh wants satisfaction *now*, wants success *now*, wants accolades *now*. **A priority, on the other hand, is about the big picture.** A priority is not about the *now*, but about the *long term.*

Esau was hungry *now*. Work hits you *now*. Someone calls you *now*—and it seems so right to respond. You're always there to jump in and help. Everyone thinks you're so great, but your home is suffering. Your life is suffering.

You have to draw the boundary lines and learn how to keep the *now* needs from usurping your long-term priorities.

Without a firm foundation built on God's wisdom, you'll give up your priorities for the cravings of your flesh. You'll give up the potential of finishing first for some fleeting victory that only leads to ruin in the end.

You have to see the big picture and value what God values. There will always be pressing needs around you. As the pastor of a large church, there are always pressing needs around me. But I've got one wife, two children, and only one lifetime to get it right!

Don't let pressing needs take precedence over your priorities.

It's not about your desires. It's about what God desires for you. Sometimes the greatest thing you can do is to say, "Someone else can take care of that pressing need right now. I'm going to make the Lord, my spouse, and my family my priority."

> *Don't let pressing needs take precedence over your priorities.*

Jesus Christ made us His priority. His *now* need was to come down off the cross. Avoiding the pain was His pressing need. But He didn't come down. The joy of our redemption was His priority.

PRIORITY POSSESSES YOUR DESTINY

We've all heard that Jacob was a trickster and a deceiver. But I'd like to challenge you right now to let every message you've ever heard about Jacob like that go. Set your mental pictures of Jacob, Esau, and their father aside for a moment because I don't want you to miss what God wants you to see.

When Esau sold the birthright, he knew full well what he was giving up. The man from the garage sale at *Antiques Roadshow*, he didn't know what he was trading. But Esau *knew* that contained in the birthright was the right to be the leader of his family and to have the double-portion blessing of the inheritance.

But Esau was not the only one who knew what was going on.

God had already seen Jacob and Esau's end from the beginning, and God *knew* that Esau would sell what God had promised for that bowl of soup! It was for that reason—before Jacob was ever born—that God told Rebekah Jacob was going to be the leader of the family.

> *And the Lord said to her… "And the older shall serve the younger."*
>
> *Genesis 25:23 NKJV*

But Isaac, the boys' father, was stubborn. He didn't want to give Jacob what *Isaac already knew* God had promised to Jacob.

Let me prove it to you.

> *Now it came to pass, when Isaac was old… that he called Esau his older son and said to him, "My son… Behold now, I am old. I do not know the day of my death. Now therefore… go out to the field and hunt game for me. And make me savory food, such as I love, and bring it to me that I may eat, that my soul may bless you before I die."*
>
> *Genesis 27:1–4 NKJV*

> ## *The things of God don't come to the passive. They come to the persistent.*

This happened *twenty-seven years after* Esau sold Jacob the birthright! Yet Isaac was trying to keep what God had promised away from Jacob and stop what God had said from coming to pass.

As a matter of fact, Isaac wasn't even dying at all. He would go on after that to live forty-three more years! This wasn't his dying declaration! Isaac just wanted to keep the promise and the blessing of the birthright from coming to Jacob!

When Jacob found out about this plot, I'm sure he said to himself, *Hey, the birthright is rightfully mine! Esau sold it to me. God said I would have it, and I bought it fair and square!*

Jacob wasn't about to give up God's promise.

BE TENACIOUS LIKE JACOB

Jacob knew that the birthright was his. He paid for it, and Esau didn't even want it, so Jacob and Rebekah came up with a plan to get what was rightfully his. In Genesis 27, Jacob said this to his mother:

> *Perhaps my father will feel me, and I shall SEEM to be a deceiver to him....*
>
> Genesis 27:12 NKJV [Author's Emphasis]

Why didn't Jacob say, "And I shall *BE* a deceiver"?

Because he wasn't!

Jacob was saying, *"It may SEEM to my father that I deceived him, but I didn't. I'm just going to get what's rightfully mine."*

Friend, you should want what's rightfully yours and what God has promised you. You should make it your highest priority to get it. A great price was paid for it.

Health, strength, joy, peace, love, and your household being saved are rightfully yours because God promised it, and Jesus paid for it!

Sometimes people will come up to me and say, "The Bible doesn't work."

But I'm telling you there's nothing wrong with God's promises.

The question is: Just how badly do you want them?

The enemy is always trying to keep them from you. The devil is defeated, but he's still putting up a fight.

When the enemy bring sickness your way, you can say, "No! I want my healing. A great price was paid for it." When your children aren't serving the Lord, you can say, "No! A great price was paid for me and my whole house to be saved. My children are going to serve the Lord." You can say, "I'm going to be healthy. I'm going to be blessed. That generational curse in my bloodline, it's broken by the power of the Lord. The great price of Jesus' blood was paid for my freedom, and I'm going to have what belongs to me. I want everything God has for me!"

But you have to be tenacious like Jacob.

The things of God don't come to the passive. They come to the persistent.

Jesus asks you today: "How badly do you want what I have for you? How badly do you want your marriage to be all that I want it to be? How badly do you want your household to serve Me? How badly do you want victory in your walk with Me?"

Even when we encounter opposition, even when second-born doubts about ourselves cause us to pause, we need to drive a stake in the ground and be persistent to value and pursue all the promises of God.

We need to build our lives on the foundation of wisdom, and set the first pillar of godly priorities firmly upon it. And to these priorities, we need to add the next pillar to build a strong home: the pillar of integrity.

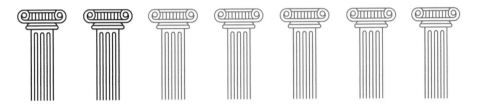

PILLAR 2
INTEGRITY

YOU CAN'T CHEAT YOUR WAY TO FIRST

I honestly believe people have painted Jacob in a bad light. They've painted him as a liar and cheat, but that wasn't really the case. Jacob valued what Esau should have valued. He valued getting all God had for him in life. Esau despised and sold his birthright for a lousy bowl of soup!

Don't blame Jacob for that!

Jacob was only going after what God had said he should have in his life. God said, "The older shall serve the younger" (Genesis 25:23 NKJV). But then for years, Isaac and Esau tried to keep Jacob from having what was rightfully his.

You can't be passive about the things of God. There is always opposition to us receiving His promises. You can't just sit back and say, "Well, if God wanted me to have a good marriage, I'd have a good marriage." "If God wanted me to have victory, I'd have it."

You have to be tenacious about going after the things God has promised to you. The enemy wants to keep them from you, but you have to go after God's will for you and your household and make it your priority.

Another key to getting all that God has for us is to build our lives with the second pillar of integrity.

RAISING UP A STANDARD

> *Do not be overcome by evil, but overcome evil with good.*
>
> *Romans 12:21 NKJV*

> *...When the enemy comes in like a flood, the Spirit of the Lord will lift up a standard against him.*
>
> *Isaiah 59:19 NKJV*

When the tide of evil tries to erode your home, your family, your business, and your walk with God, the Lord will raise up a standard and break the waves that are trying to come against you. We can never overcome evil with more evil. The only thing that will turn the tide is God's standard of integrity.

So, what does integrity look like today? Is it simply keeping your word? Doing what you say you're going to do? That certainly is one sign of godly integrity, but that's only part of what integrity truly is.

Integrity is consistently doing the right thing at the right time for the right reason.

This world needs people of integrity—people who will stand on the foundation of wisdom with their priorities set on what God values, people who will consistently do the right thing because it's the right thing to do. When we build our lives with the pillar of integrity, God will come to our aid.

To understand the deeper concept behind the meaning of integrity, it helps to look at the word itself. The root of the English word is the word *integer*, which means *intact* or *whole*. From your school days, you may remember that integers are whole numbers. A fraction is not an integer. It's not seven-eighths or one and a half. An integer is a *whole* number.

As a follower of Christ, a life of integrity means following the whole of God's Word—not seven-eighths of it, or some smaller portion. A life of integrity means you won't add to or take away from what God has said, trying to turn the truth into something subjective from the world. To some, holding this high standard may seem impossible, but God doesn't ask for perfection. Only He is perfect, but when it comes to integrity, He's looking at the intents of our hearts.

INTEGRITY REQUIRES REVELATION

After Isaac blessed Jacob with the birthright he rightfully owned because Esau had sold it to him, God's plan to make their family a great nation required a next step: Jacob needed a wife. And not just any wife. Isaac directed Jacob to travel about thirty miles away, where Jacob was told to find a wife among his uncle Laban's daughters.

It was on this journey that Jacob had his dream about the ladder to Heaven. Jacob was headed to find a wife, but he was also running away from Esau, and he didn't have time to even carry his bedding with him. Stopping in the desert for the night, Jacob rested his head on a rock and drifted off to sleep. Starting with a vision of angels ascending and descending on the ladder, Jacob then saw the Lord, who affirmed His promise:

> *I am the Lord, the God of your father Abraham and the God of Isaac. I will give you and your descendants the land on which you are lying.... All peoples on earth will be blessed through you and your offspring. I am with you and will watch over you wherever you go, and I will bring you back to this land. I will not leave you until I have done what I have promised you.*
>
> *Genesis 28:13–15 NIV*

I used to read that passage as if it were conditional. Have you ever made a conditional vow with God? Something like, "God, if You'll just bail me out of this one, then I promise I'll serve You after that."

The first time I read this, I thought that's what Jacob was doing. It sounded like he was making his vow to God conditional, "Lord, *if* You'll help me out of this mess, *then* I'll serve You and pay my tithes."

Integrity is consistently doing the right thing at the right time for the right reason.

But as I studied it further, I realized that's not was Jacob was saying at all. He was saying, "If *God loves me* the way He says He loves me, and *He'll do all the things He promised me*, and *He is who He says He is,* then *how could I NOT serve Him?* I'd be a fool if I don't make Him my God forever and do whatever He says."

Jacob served God out of revelation, not out of condition.

How do I know? Because verse 18 says he set up an altar right then and there. Early in the morning Jacob got up and built an altar from the rock he had used as a pillow where he had slept, and he poured oil on it.

You see, in Old Testament times, an altar was a pillar set up to mark a place where you presented what was yours to the Lord so that you could receive what was His. And that purpose remains today.

Jacob was saying, because of how good God is, no longer am I going to try to do this with my thoughts, but I'm going to receive His thoughts—no longer my ways, but His ways—no longer my integrity, but His integrity. Jacob said, "God is going to be my standard, and I'm going to serve Him completely."

> *God is going to be my standard, and I'm going to serve Him completely.*

I'm so grateful God takes what is ours and gives us what is His!

We don't have to live by our standards or the world's standards. We're going to take up God's standard and live in integrity so that He can use us as a light to overcome the darkness of this world. We're going to serve Him out of revelation—not conditionally, only when we feel like it. We're going to serve Him because He is righteous. He is good. He is loving, and He is faithful to do everything He has promised!

You can make your own altar to the living God today, not with stones or with tables in your home surrounded by pictures of Jesus and burning incense. No, you can make an altar in your heart—a place where you exchange your standards for God's.

As Jacob teaches us, there's a big difference between God's ways and the world's.

YOUR INTEGRITY IS NOT CONTINGENT ON CIRCUMSTANCES

When Jacob arrived at the place where his maternal relatives lived, it didn't take long for him to meet one of Laban's daughters. A shepherd for her father, Rachel had brought her sheep to the same well Jacob had stopped at. Wanting to make a good impression, he rolled away the stone that covered the well, which was quite a feat, since it normally took several people to move it. Jacob watered Rachel's sheep for her, and then he kissed her. He was overjoyed about the meeting God had orchestrated.

After Jacob had stayed at his uncle's home for a month, Laban said, "Just because you are a relative of mine, should you work for me for nothing? Tell me what your wages should be."

Rather than a paycheck, Jacob countered with a request that was more long term, in more ways than one. "I'll work for you seven years in return for your younger daughter, Rachel."

Laban agreed, and we're told Jacob did indeed serve his uncle seven years for Rachel's hand in marriage (Genesis 29:15–20 NKJV).

The wedding day came, but Laban pulled a fast one. He had his older daughter, Leah, stand in as the bride on the wedding night! Back then, the bride usually had her entire face covered with a veil that only had a small opening for the eyes. Jacob didn't know he had been duped until the next morning. He woke up and was shocked to roll over and find he was married to the wrong daughter!

> *What is this you have done to me? Was it not for Rachel that I served you? Why then have you deceived me?*
>
> *Genesis 29:25 NKJV*

Jacob protested loudly, but Laban defended himself by saying, "It is not our custom here to give the younger daughter in marriage before the older one." In other words, "Didn't you see that in the fine print on page six of the contract?"

I can only imagine that things must have gotten pretty heated at that point, so to calm Jacob down, Laban told him, "Finish the first daughter's bridal week; then I'll give you the younger one also—in return for another seven years of work" (Genesis 29:26–27 NKJV).

If you were in Jacob's shoes, what would you do?

Most people would say, "Laban tricked me, why should I stick around and serve him seven more years? I'll just wait for the moment when I can whisk Rachel away, and we'll be out of here!"

But that's not what Jacob did. **Godly integrity is not contingent on what others do or on the situation in which you find yourself.** Jacob's integrity wasn't based on what Laban did. Jacob was intent on remaining a man of his word. He said, "I'll do it. I'll serve you for another seven years." Even though Laban tricked him, Jacob swore to his own hurt and served Laban an extra seven years for the wife he wanted.

Integrity is not about being right. It's about doing right.

INTEGRITY SPEAKS FOR ITSELF

The pressures of life, situational ethics, disappointments in what people do or don't do—that's how the world sets their standards. But integrity sets the standard according to what God says.

Some years ago, when our church was embarking on a building program to meet the needs of our growing congregation and outreach efforts to the community, I was invited to speak at another church. A member of that congregation picked me up at the airport and was my host during those three days. Judging from his sporty car, I could tell he was affluent. And sure enough, I learned from our conversation that he was a successful businessman.

Later, during a bit of free time, this man invited me to his home and said he'd appreciate it if I would pray with him about something. He explained that he wanted to sell one of his businesses and mentioned that he was hoping it would go for $70 million. Then he surprised me by saying, "Pastor, I really like what you and your church are doing in Destin. When I sell my business, I want to tithe to your building program from the sale proceeds. Will you pray with me about that?"

I silently gulped. A tithe on that would be $7 million. Immediately I started thinking about all the stress a contribution like that would take off of me and our congregation. I thought about it for a second, but then I knew exactly what to do.

"No sir," I said. "I will gladly pray about the sale of your business, but the tithe off of that belongs to your local church. It belongs in your storehouse, not mine."

Your integrity will speak for you. When you do the right thing at the right time for the right reason, God will promote you. You can hold onto God's standards at all times and watch the flood waters dissipate.

Jacob put it this way:

> *And my honesty will testify for me in the future...*
>
> *Genesis 30:33 NIV*

God calls us to be people of integrity for His sake, but it also benefits us and others.

For the Lord God is a sun and shield; The Lord will give grace and glory; No good thing will He withhold from those who walk uprightly.

Psalm 84:11 NKJV

The blessing of the Lord makes one rich, and He adds no sorrow with it.

Proverbs 10:22 NKJV

Do the right thing, my friend, and watch God defend you. Do the right thing, and watch Him promote you.

When you walk uprightly and are consistently honest, people around you can trust you. Your spouse can trust you. Your children can trust you. Coworkers can trust you. All because they know you will choose integrity, no matter what others may do. The world's way is to defend yourself, to promote yourself, to get ahead no matter the cost. **But you can't cheat your way to the top.**

> *Do the right thing, and watch God promote you.*

Even after Laban deceived Jacob to get seven more years of work from him, Laban continued his underhanded ways, cheating Jacob by changing his wages ten times (Genesis 31:7). But in the end, Jacob still got his blessing.

After working for Laban fourteen years, Jacob approached his father-in-law with a proposal. He wanted to go back to his homeland.

> *Jacob said to him, "You know how I have worked for you and how your livestock has fared under my care. The little you had before I came has increased greatly, and the Lord has blessed you wherever I have been. But now, when may I do something for my own household?"*

Genesis 30:29–30 NIV

Jacob went on to ask Laban if he could have all the speckled, spotted, and dark-colored sheep in the flock, and Laban agreed to the arrangement.

Now, I don't know a lot about sheep, but this seems like one of the most lopsided trades in ranching history. (The only black sheep I've ever seen were the ones at our family reunion!) But still Jacob made this deal with Laban. He said, "Every white sheep will be yours, but the black ones will be mine. Every solid-colored goat will be yours, and every striped or speckled one will be mine. My honesty will speak for me in the future. God will make sure my integrity is rewarded. Let God be God and vindicate me if I've done the right thing" (Genesis 30:31–33 NIV).

Under Jacob's care God's blessing was evident. Jacob's part of the flock flourished, and in the end it vastly outnumbered Laban's part.

Jacob exhibited integrity time and time again. He did the right thing for the right reasons for a long time.

Integrity is not a flash of brilliance. It's a model of consistency.

Godly integrity was a pillar in Jacob's life that affected all the generations to come. Ultimately, that's why the Lord wants us to live with integrity. When we operate in integrity it brings us authority, which leads to influence.

INTEGRITY BRINGS AUTHORITY AND INFLUENCE

One of the best-known sections in the Bible is Jesus' Sermon on the Mount. Found in Matthew's gospel, chapters five through seven, it presents the Lord's teachings on a variety of topics, from prayer and fasting, to loving our enemies and even the pitfalls of worrying too much. Jesus, still early on in His ministry, clearly influenced the crowds. Just look at how the entire Scripture passage concludes:

> *So it was, when Jesus had ended these sayings, that the people were astonished at His teaching, for He taught them as one having authority, and not as the scribes.*
>
> *Matthew 7:28–29 NKJV*

You see, the scribes at that time, experts in Jewish laws and leaders in the community, were known for telling people, "Do this" and "Do that," but they were not following the rules themselves. The religious leaders of the day didn't have any authority because they taught the Law but didn't live it. They were far from trustworthy, and because of this they lacked influence.

There are a lot of very gifted people in the world who don't walk in authority. They like to look important on the outside, but they don't have any real influence.

Jesus was different. People knew His "yes" meant yes, and His "no" meant no (Matthew 5:37). He walked in the whole truth, and His integrity gave Him great authority with God and with men.

It's with integrity that we gain influence. As people see us walking in submission to God no matter what our circumstances—as they see that we are people who do the right thing at the right time for the right reason, they'll see we can be trusted, and they'll want what we have.

The apostle Paul had the same revelation. He was driven by one thing: to influence people for Christ. Paul went to great lengths to not only spread the gospel but also to avoid compromising it. It's impossible to miss his passion:

> *What is my reward then? That when I preach the gospel, I may present the gospel of Christ without charge, that I may not abuse my authority in the gospel.*
>
> *1 Corinthians 9:18 NKJV*

If we are inconsistent in how we live, if we're out of balance because of unhealthy excesses, our authority and influence will surely crumble. But if we build our lives and homes with the godly pillar of integrity, God will see to it that we have influence and are greatly blessed.

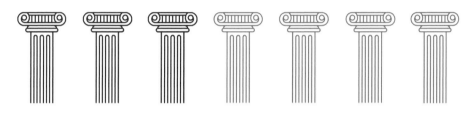

PILLAR 3
LOYALTY

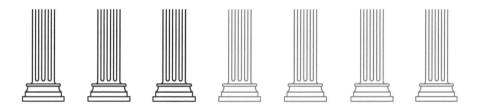

LOYALTY

PILLAR OF SUCCESSFUL RELATIONSHIPS

Friends in other parts of the country sometimes give Jackie and me a hard time about living in such a beautiful part of the Florida Panhandle. What can I say? We were simply being obedient when God called us to Destin, known as "the world's luckiest fishing village." I should clarify. For many decades it was a small fishing village. Nowadays, Destin is still a relatively small city population-wise, but when word got out about our white beaches—among the whitest in the world—touched by the emerald green waters of the Gulf of Mexico, people started visiting our little part of the world in droves. In fact, more than three million visitors spend time here each year.

As you might expect, our area—touted as the Emerald Coast—is now home to many resorts, hotels, and other businesses to accommodate all the visitors. One thing I have noticed here and certainly elsewhere is that many of those businesses have customer loyalty programs. Whether it's the airlines that fly people here, the hotels, or the corner coffee shops, they all try their best to attract and reward frequent customers.

I get why they call them "loyalty programs," but their definition of loyalty is nothing like what we see in the Bible, and it's far from the godly loyalty that forms the third pillar in the life of a strong Christian.

Buy nine pizzas and the tenth is free!

Join our car wash club—get $2 off our regular price!

Expedited car rentals for members!

Yes, this is why our pockets and purses are overflowing with plastic cards and key fobs. Businesses want our loyalty, and we want a deal. There's nothing wrong with this, but it's hardly the type of loyalty that changes lives. As Jacob and others in the Bible show us, true loyalty pleases God and has amazing effects.

In fact, **loyalty is the pillar of successful relationships**.

LOYALTY ALWAYS MAKES THE BEST OFFER

When we left Jacob's story in the last chapter, he was overseeing his expanding, eye-catching flocks of multi-colored sheep, while still serving his father-in-law, Laban. God saw how honest and loyal Jacob had been throughout all those years, and told him, "Go back to the land of your fathers and to your relatives, and I will be with you" (Genesis 31:3 NIV). Jacob told Rachel and Leah about the Lord's command and then made his case for why they should leave for Canaan without even telling Laban.

> ...I see your father's countenance, that it is not favorable toward me as before; but the God of my father has been with me. And you know that with all my might I have served your father. Yet your father has deceived me and changed my wages ten times, but God did not allow him to hurt me.
>
> Genesis 31:5–7 NKJV

This brief passage provides these key points related to loyalty:

» **Jacob served Laban with all his might.**

» **Jacob did this even though Laban treated him poorly.**

» **God rewarded Jacob for his loyalty.**

Like godly integrity, which is consistently honest (not seven-eighths "honest"), godly loyalty doesn't hold anything back. **True loyalty makes the best offer and makes it first.** Loyalty doesn't say, "I'll hold back my best until I see how you respond." No, loyalty says, "I'll give you all I can give, no matter what you do or don't do in return."

That's what Jacob did for Laban. He gave his father-in-law twenty years of hard work. He gave Laban his best. As a shepherd, probably working alone in remote fields, I imagine Jacob could have slacked off. Or, he could have secretly sold a few of Laban's sheep once in a while to build up his own wealth. But he didn't. Jacob loyally served Laban with all his might.

What makes this all the more remarkable, especially to our human eyes, is that Jacob served Laban faithfully despite Laban's conniving ways. For the first fourteen years of their relationship, Jacob was essentially an indentured servant to Laban, and for the six years that followed that, Laban changed Jacob's agreed-upon wages ten different times!

I don't know about you, but that seems a bit over the top to me. It's one thing to return someone's loyalty, it's quite another when your loyalty is not reciprocated.

> *True loyalty makes the best offer and makes it first.*

Perhaps you can relate. Maybe your efforts at work are being overlooked. Or, maybe at home, or even as a volunteer at church, do you sometimes wonder, *When is someone going to acknowledge what I'm doing? When is all my hard work going to pay off?*

Our Lord Jesus knows all about unreturned loyalty. When He died for us, we weren't worshipping Him and praising Him for all He was doing. The Bible tells us that Christ died for us *while we were still sinners* (Romans 5:8).

Loyalty makes the best offer, regardless of what is offered in return.

Our Lord's death was not quick or painless. It was a slow, violent process. In all, He bled in seven different ways to save and redeem us.

1. His sweat turned to blood in Gethsemane so we could find relief from the pressure and stresses of life.

2. He was whipped on His back so that by those bloody stripes we could be healed.

3. He bled from His head from the crown of thorns so we could have peace of mind.

4. He bled from His hands so our hands could prosper.

5. He bled from His feet so we could have direction for our lives.

6. He was pierced in His side (His heart) so our hearts could be made whole.

7. He was bruised all over, bleeding under His skin, for our iniquities.

Jesus didn't die just to save us a little bit. He gave us His all. He paid the ultimate price to save us, heal us, and free us. That's absolute loyalty.

Why did He do it? Because Jesus knew His loyalty that day on the cross would purchase something far greater in the future—it would buy back His Church.

YOUR FUTURE IS TIED TO YOUR LOYALTY TODAY

Just as Jesus knew His momentary pain would purchase a bright and glorious future, your loyalty today is determining your future. One way or the other, you're setting yourself up for what's ahead in your life through the loyalty you're showing to God and to the people with whom you're in relationship.

Let's pick up where we left off a few pages back and see how this principle was set into motion in Jacob's story.

> *And you know that with all my might I have served your father.*
> *Yet your father has deceived me and changed my wages ten times,*
> *but God did not allow him to hurt me…. So God has taken away*
> *the livestock of your father and given them to me.*
>
> *Genesis 31:6–7, 9 NKJV*

I've seen it time and again: Loyalty will wane if we are expecting people to reward us. As imperfect creatures, people will disappoint us. They won't always recognize or value our dedication.

Let me urge you to look instead to God for His rewards. He knows how faithful you are. Trust Him to repay you in the future for your loyalty today.

> *God is not unjust; he will not forget your work and the love you*
> *have shown him as you have helped his people and continue to*
> *help them.*
>
> *Hebrews 6:10 NIV*

Don't stop being loyal and committed because of what some person didn't do for you. God is looking out for you. If you're in a dead-end job, you might think, *I can only go as far as my boss allows.* But your boss is only in charge of so much. We serve a God who is in charge of everything!

Don't sit around and wait for someone else to do their part before you do your part. Give first—and give your all! If your spouse or your family doesn't appreciate all you do, keep giving. If your friends don't reciprocate your loyalty toward them, keep giving. For your family's sake, for your friends' sake, for God's sake, stay loyal and committed. You will be rewarded. The God who sees all and gave all will take care of you!

When Jacob and his family slipped away to return to Canaan, Laban felt betrayed and took off after Jacob's caravan. When Laban caught up to Jacob, he was angry, but he explained that because God had spoken to him in a dream the night before, he wouldn't harm his son-in-law.

Jacob was hardly concerned. He knew he was in the right, and he made sure Laban knew why he had prospered:

> If the God of my father, the God of Abraham and the Fear of Isaac, had not been with me, you would surely have sent me away empty-handed. But God has seen my hardship and the toil of my hands, and last night he rebuked you.
>
> Genesis 31:42 NIV

God helped Jacob and protected him. He experienced what his descendant, David, would later express so confidently:

> The Lord is my strength and my shield; my heart trusted in Him, and I am helped....
>
> Psalm 28:7 NKJV

God intervened on Jacob's behalf, but can you imagine working for Laban for twenty years and walking away with nothing? If Laban had had his way, that's what would have happened.

Relationships shouldn't be like that.

LOYALTY WORKS BOTH WAYS

A friend of mine is an experienced mountain climber. When he described how he climbed with a partner, it immediately struck me as a picture of godly loyalty.

The climbing details are quite involved and depend on the situation. But basically, when climbing in pairs, one climber scales a section of rock alone until reaching a good stopping point. There he hammers an anchor into the rock and ties himself off to the anchor with a rope. Then he lowers a safety rope to his climbing partner and helps him up to the higher spot.

That first climber, having done most of the work so far, now lets his partner free climb to the next level, where the second man sets a new anchor and ties himself off. On up the mountain the partners take turns climbing to the next level, helping each other up and then beyond.

That's how loyalty should be—that's how every relationship should be—back and forth effort, with each person doing his or her part.

Are you doing your part in the relationships you have? Are you loyal?

Many of our relationships are like those between climbing partners, where one person is seemingly "above" the other. If you manage others at work, are you loyal to your staff? Loyalty not only goes up to those who are above us in position or authority, loyalty must also go down to those we are responsible for, too.

> *Are you doing your part in the relationships you have? Are you loyal?*

If you're a parent, you certainly expect obedience and loyalty from your children. But are you loyal to them? Do you spend quality time with them? Are you in their corner cheering them on, even when they make poor decisions? If you're a husband, do you love and nurture your wife? If you're a wife, do you honor and respect your husband?

When I perform wedding ceremonies, I often explain how a godly marriage is a *covenant*, not a *contract*. When you enter into a *contract*, you say, in effect, "These are the rights I want to protect. These are the responsibilities I want to limit. And if you don't uphold your end of the agreement, it will be null and void." A *covenant*, on the other hand, says, "I give up all my rights; I will be responsible for anything and everything this relationship requires, regardless of what life brings us or how you treat me—for as long as we both shall live."

While marriage is a commitment for life, no one is more committed to you than God. His loyalty to His children stretches from the beginning of time and beyond into eternity. He is not in a contract relationship with us. It is a covenant sealed with the blood of Jesus Christ. As such, we should understand that loyalty with God works both ways. He gave His all to us, and He's looking for nothing less in return.

DON'T TAKE YOUR RELATIONSHIPS FOR GRANTED

I wish you could meet my father-in-law. Talk about a loyal man—he is a star in that regard.

Years ago, when phone companies like AT&T, Sprint, and a company called MCI were competing fiercely for customers, my father-in-law got a sales call at home. "We will give you $75 to switch your phone service to AT&T," the rep told him. When my father-in-law politely let her know he already was an AT&T customer, she apologized for the mix-up and started to wrap up the call.

"Wait," he interrupted. "You're offering how much to new customers?" When she repeated the $75 amount, he responded, "Well, what are you going to give me—a loyal AT&T customer—someone who's never left you at all?"

Don't you already love the guy?

A bit flustered the woman answered, "Hmm. I've never been asked that before. Let me look into it and call you back."

Sure enough, that AT&T rep called him again, and in no time my father-in-law was enjoying three free months of local and long-distance phone service.

But the story doesn't end there.

I was a loyal AT&T customer, too! And when I heard about my father-in-law's deal, I rang up AT&T and asked what I could expect for being a loyal customer. I got the same initial response as my father-in-law. "I've never been asked that," the rep informed me.

"Well," I said, "let me tell you what a man down in Orlando got...." A few days later, I was enjoying three free months of service at my house, too!

Yes, the best kind of loyalty goes both ways. But what if you find yourself not feeling all that loyal to a certain person in your life? Or, what if you'd like someone to be more loyal to you?

Can anything help?

THOUGHTFULNESS AND THANKFULNESS INSPIRE LOYALTY

This isn't a big secret, but it's something we don't recognize enough: Thankfulness and thoughtfulness are a powerful tandem. I've seen them inspire loyalty in others, as well as, in my own heart.

I am so thankful for the pastor who mentored me early in my ministry. After working for him for several years, he could have been like Laban and could have discouraged me from doing anything but continue to serve him at his church. Instead, he poured himself into me, so that one day I would be ready to lead my own church. And when that time came, he didn't send me off emptyhanded. No, he blessed me with the funds for three months' rent and six months' salary. I was already loyal to my pastor, but his kindness cemented it.

> *Lord, don't let us be the kind of people who aren't thoughtful or thankful to everyone who has made a difference in our lives!*

When you look around your company, do you realize that you wouldn't be there without your employees or your boss? Or when you look at your family, maybe your spouse nursed you back to health when you were sick or he or she encouraged you through a tough time in your life. Are you thankful for all they have done? Maybe your friends helped you with a problem you had with your children or helped you to recover from a bad situation at work.

When you think about all the people around you, I encourage you not to think, *What have you done for me lately?* Instead think, *What have you done for me?* and then show them just how thankful you are.

As you think about being thankful in your relationships, I'd like you to also consider the most important one—your relationship with God. Stop and think about all the Lord has done for you, and turn your thoughtfulness into thankfulness. Whenever your faith needs a boost, take time to recall His goodness toward you.

The psalmist writes:

> *Bless the Lord, O my soul; And all that is within me, bless His holy name! Bless the Lord, O my soul, And forget not all His benefits.*
>
> *Psalm 103:1–2 NKJV*

Your thoughts and thankfulness will inspire you to be even more loyal to Him.

LOYALTY PROTECTS AND PROVIDES

Let's go back to Jacob's story and look at another aspect of true loyalty. Jacob wouldn't allow Laban to suffer loss.

> *I have been with you for twenty years now. Your sheep and goats have not miscarried, nor have I eaten rams from your flocks. I did not bring you animals torn by wild beasts; I bore the loss myself. And you demanded payment from me for whatever was stolen by day or night.*
>
> *Genesis 31:38–39 NIV*

Even though Laban was deceitful and unfaithful to Jacob, Jacob suffered loss himself, rather than allowing his father-in-law to be harmed.

Talk about faithful. Jacob's attitude was, "It's not about me and my gain. It's about you." God blesses that kind of faithfulness.

Think about all the Lord has done for you, and turn your thoughtfulness into thankfulness.

This kind of loyalty epitomizes the idea that you can never be too loyal—an exceptional trait seen in a select few in the Bible. One such person was the "beloved disciple" of Jesus, the Apostle John. John was the only disciple of the twelve who was present at Christ's crucifixion. As Jesus was dying, He asked John to care for His mother. Given the anger many people had for Jesus and His followers at the time, the request had to be a burden—possibly even risky— but John, the loyal friend of Jesus, took Mary into his own home from that day forward (John 19:27).

Another incredible model of godly loyalty in the Bible is David. Although there was a point in David's life when Saul was out to destroy him, David always remained loyal to his king. When David was hiding in the wilderness, God caused Saul and his guards to come into situations where David could have easily taken Saul's life (1 Samuel 24). After all, Saul had disobeyed the Lord, and he knew his kingdom was coming to an end. It would have been a simple thing for David to kill Saul in the valley or in the cave and take the throne God had promised to give him. But David was too loyal for that.

I imagine David was tempted to think, *No one's going to think of me, if I don't think of myself.* Make no mistake, there will be times in all our lives when we'll be tempted to think like that. But if we'll just remain loyal no matter what—on the other side of that test is the blessing of God. David's loyalty prevented him from catapulting himself to the forefront by causing someone else's loss. David passed his test, and God promoted him at just the right time.

YOU CAN TRUST GOD'S LOYALTY

There are two things we need to ask ourselves when we look at the stories of these faithful men in the Bible. First, "Am I the kind of person who is loyal to protect others and provide for them even if it costs me something?" And second, "Do I have that kind of person in my life?" If the answer to both questions is yes, you're perfectly positioned for a tremendous blessing from God.

> *There is no one more loyal or committed to you than God.*

God is going to look out for you. He's going to be faithful to you. **There is no one more loyal or committed to you than God.**

God told Jacob, "Return to the land of your fathers and to your family, and I will be with you" (Genesis 31:3 NKJV). That was a promise from God for Jacob, but Jesus made the same promise to us.

> *...And surely I am with you always, to the very end of the age.*
>
> *Matthew 28:20 NIV*

> *...For He Himself has said, "I will never leave you nor forsake you."*
>
> *Hebrews 13:5 NKJV*

Beloved, that's your promise from God. He'll be with you. He'll be your shield and exceeding great reward. He will never ever leave you. **He will be faithful to you until the end of eternity. No matter what.**

> *If we are unfaithful, he remains faithful, for he cannot deny who he is.*
>
> *2 Timothy 2:13 NLT*

Even when we can't see how it's going to bless us to stay faithful to Him and to others, God is still loyal to us, and He will make a way.

When you're loyal in your relationships, God looks down and takes note.

You can trust God to be loyal to you. And as you're loyal to Him today, you'll see His reward in your tomorrows.

PILLAR 4
LOVE

LOVE

THE FIVE ASPECTS OF LOVE

We have priorities, integrity, and loyalty on the right side, and accountability, righteousness, and stewardship on the left. And the pillar of love sits squarely in the middle of a strong and godly house.

Love is at the center of it all, because love holds everything together.

If we model the love of Christ in our homes, our families will be strong. If we model His love in our friendships, in our jobs, and in our everyday interactions, people will notice and be drawn to the Lord.

The kingdom of Heaven is the strongest force in the universe—the Bible says it's unshakeable and cannot be moved (Hebrews 12:28). Why is it so strong? Because Love is there in the center of it.

God is love (1 John 4:8).

The Bible's "love chapter" (1 Corinthians 13) beautifully teaches us what love is and what it isn't. Love is patient. Love is kind. Love is unselfish, not proud, and more. From this passage and from the story of Jacob in the Scriptures, I see five different facets to the pillar of love that the Lord wants to help us embody to build strong lives.

EXCLUSIVE LOVE

It's a sad fact of life: The world teaches us that we need to "perform" in order to be accepted and loved. Your son's teacher may love having him in class, but the teacher's attitude might cool if your son doesn't do his schoolwork. If you work in sales, your boss may appreciate your wit and your charisma, that is, as long as you perform and meet the company's sales goals every month.

We can't escape it. The world is performance oriented. But the good news is, God doesn't operate this way.

God's love for us is exclusive. When it comes to His love for us, it doesn't matter what we do or don't do. His love is unconditional.

Exclusive love values the person over the performance.

...He made us accepted in the Beloved.

Ephesians 1:6 NKJV

God loves us and accepts us unconditionally, and He wants us to love Him and others unconditionally, in return. God loves us for who we are, not for what we've done.

> *Godly love always motivates. It never intimidates.*

Everyone needs someone who loves them just for who they are. We all need a place of refuge and acceptance.

Our homes need to be places where people are loved unconditionally. Certainly there are times when we need to speak words of correction, but we should never withhold our love based on someone's performance. Our families need to hear us say, "I accept you for who you are, not just for what you've done."

Godly love always motivates. It never intimidates.

It isn't demanding and controlling. "You need to do this or else!" No, godly love excludes all conditions and loves without expectations to perform.

I know my wife loves me unconditionally. Jackie doesn't pressure me to do this or that... or else she'll remove her love This doesn't mean I'm off the hook and can neglect her. Quite the opposite, I try to be the best husband I can be, because I am motivated by her love, not intimidated to achieve.

We should strive to give our all to our spouses and families; however, we cannot do it *FOR* love—to try to earn love in return—but we do it *FROM* love—out of a place where we know we are already loved and accepted by God.

This kind of exclusive love takes the pressure off relationships. Perhaps that's how Jacob could serve his father-in-law for seven years for Rachel, and yet:

> ...*They seemed only **a few days** to him **because of the love** he had for her.*
>
> *Genesis 29:20 NIV [Author's Emphasis]*

Doesn't that just sound like it belongs in a Hallmark card?

Before Rachel ever cooked a meal for him, before she ever did a load of laundry, before she ever gave him that backrub he was wanting—Jacob loved her, and he served her.

Everyone needs that kind of love. Your home needs to be a place of refuge. Your spouse and kids need to know they can walk in the door, and you'll say, "I don't care what you did today. I love you for who you are."

That's where you'll grow and flourish, with that kind of love—an exclusive love that's all yours, just because of who you are.

Even Jesus, the Son of God, needed acceptance.

> *You are My beloved Son; in You I am well pleased.*
>
> *Luke 3:22 NKJV*

Jesus hadn't even started His ministry yet. He hadn't turned water into wine or healed a single blind man. He hadn't defeated the devil in the wilderness. Jesus hadn't "performed" yet, but the Father's words to His Son were encouraging. He wasn't giving Jesus a list of things He had to do to earn acceptance. The Father's words motivated Jesus to be all that He could be.

And Jesus took that motivating love into the wilderness to fight the enemy of His soul. The Holy Spirit led Jesus into the wilderness, where He fasted for forty days, and true to form, the enemy came on the scene to challenge Him.

> *"If you are the Son of God," he said, "throw yourself down from here."*
>
> *Luke 4:10 NIV*

Did you catch it? It's very subtle.

Satan dropped the word "beloved" from how God had described Jesus. The devil was trying to get Jesus to question what the Father said. *Am I the beloved Son? Am I accepted?*

Then the enemy said in so many words, "If you are the Son... PERFORM! Turn this stone into bread. Jump off this pinnacle. Prove you are accepted by God!"

Jesus' simple response is one we can also employ: "I don't have to prove it. I know I am beloved by My Father. Now get out of here!"

That's the way God wants us to be. When we know we are loved unconditionally we can extend that love to others.

Exclusive love is powerful, especially for breaking through to people who think they are unlovable.

That's how the Prodigal Son saw himself. Luke 15 describes a young man desperate to escape the pit of sin he had fallen into after leaving home and squandering his father's inheritance. The world had chewed him up when the Lord started to get through to his heart. The young man knew he needed to repent for his sins, but he wondered, could he go home? Deep down, he must have believed his father would accept him back, at least he hoped he would. And "when he was still a great way off, his father saw him and had compassion, and ran and fell on his neck and kissed him" (Luke 15:20 NKJV).

If you are close to someone trapped in sin, maybe even a family member like the Prodigal Son, tough love may be necessary, but never underestimate the ability of exclusive love to change a person's heart.

INCLUSIVE LOVE

Jacob's story in Genesis demonstrates the importance of a second kind of love: *inclusive love*. Jacob experienced the hard truth that **affection and honor should never be divided.**

With two wives, it was inevitable that Jacob's heart would be divided. His affection for Rachel was clear the moment they first met, and he noticed she was "beautiful of form and appearance" (Genesis 29:17 NKJV).

We don't have to guess how Jacob felt about Leah. The Bible makes that clear.

...And his love for Rachel was greater than his love for Leah.

Genesis 29:30 NIV

There are two really important principles here I want you to notice:

1. **We give our affection to that which gives us our identity.** During their marriage, Jacob did indeed love Rachel the most. She was God's first chosen wife for him; she gave him his identity. And it was her firstborn son, Joseph, who would continue Jacob's lineage all the way to Jesus.

2. **We honor those who meet our needs.** Though Jacob and Leah's marriage was founded on deception, Leah gave him six sons and a daughter. For this, he honored her. How do we know he honored Leah? Years later, when she died, Jacob buried Leah in the same cave as his grandparents and parents: Abraham, Sarah, Isaac, and Rebekah. Rachel was not honored the same way. After she died giving birth to her second child, Jacob buried Rachel near Bethlehem.

> *Affection and honor should never be divided.*

We still see this connection between love and identity today. A man will often give his affection to his career, because this is where he gets his sense of identity ("I'm an attorney," "I'm a project manager," etc.). A woman may do the same with her career, or she may pour all her affection into her children, because motherhood is her identity.

We give affection to that which gives us our identity. We honor those who meet our needs.

Husbands—wives—our affection and honor should never be divided.

To be clear, it's good to care, even deeply, about your work and other worthy activities. It all depends on our priorities. But if I set my affection toward my church more than toward my wife, both would suffer. Things at church would crumble, and our home would not be strong.

If you want to have a strong home and marriage, make sure your affection and your honor are both directed toward your spouse.

In the same way, Jesus is the Lover of our souls. God doesn't just want your honor. He wants your affection, too.

> *Set your affection on things above, not on things on the earth.*
>
> *Colossians 3:2 NKJV*

> *Give honor to whom honor is due.*
>
> *Romans 13:7 KJV*

We can **give honor** and **set our affections**. This is within our power.

Jesus warned that no man can serve two masters. We will ultimately love one and hate the other (Matthew 6:24). We must choose. If our affections and honor aren't all-inclusive—when there's duplicity in our souls, we begin to divide our own homes, and they fall apart.

This truth echoed David's prayer from generations earlier.

> *Teach me your way, Lord, that I may rely on your faithfulness: give me an undivided heart, that I may fear your name. I will praise you, Lord my God, with all my heart; I will glorify your name forever.*
>
> *Psalm 86:11–12 NIV*

May this be your prayer and mine.

TENDER LOVE

The third aspect of the God kind of love is tender love. **Tender love is what springs up in you when you put yourself in another person's shoes.**

If you have a friend, a sibling, or a spouse who always "gets you"—who can empathize with what's going on in your life—you already know how special tender love is. Hopefully, you are already that kind of person, too. It's not always easy to be tender-hearted, though.

I remember not long after our marriage, Jackie and I went to a movie with our best man, John, and his wife, Lori. We saw a movie called, *The Champ*. It was the story of a washed-up boxer who attempts a comeback to give his young son a better life.

If you've never seen it, I won't give away the ending, but I will say I once saw it on a list of "all-time tear-jerker" movies. By the end of the film, my wife and Lori were weeping. I admit I was getting misty eyed, too. But John? Well, I looked over and he was just sitting there, emotionless, impatiently bouncing his leg.

"John," my wife said once she was able to collect herself a bit. "How are you not crying? Don't you have any feelings?"

"Sure, I do," he said.

When you can understand another's point of view, you'll make progress in that relationship.

Still unconvinced, Jackie asked him, "Haven't you ever cried during a movie?"

"Yes," John replied matter of factly. "I cried at the movie *Jaws*—when the shark died."

Now, in John's defense, years of friendship have shown me he does have a tender heart.

Still, as I said, it's not always easy to put ourselves in another person's shoes.

Like every good thing in life, Jesus Christ is our example, as well as, our motivation. His death on the cross was the ultimate moment of someone putting Himself in another person's shoes—your shoes and mine. Jesus was tender hearted toward us, even when while we were still sinners.

> *Who himself bore our sins in his own body on the tree, that we, having died to sins, might live for righteousness....*
>
> *1 Peter 2:24 NIV*

Because of this amazing act of love, we can now live for righteousness. We can choose to be kind and tender hearted.

> *Be kind to one another, tenderhearted, forgiving one another, even as God in Christ forgave [us].*
>
> *Ephesians 4:32 NIV*

When someone has offended you, they need your forgiveness. In the same way Christ put Himself in your shoes, put yourself in the shoes of another.

As you put yourself in a place where you can understand another person's point of view, you'll make progress in that relationship.

When I was growing up, there was a period when I wrestled with my relationship with my father. He wasn't the kind of dad who said, "Atta boy." He never said, "I'm proud of you, Steve." Instead, he would give me and my brother twenty- or fifty-dollar bills for spending money now and then, without hardly saying a word.

This got to me one day, I went to my mom and asked, "What's wrong with Dad? Why can't he just say, 'Way to go, son,' or tell me he's proud of me?"

"You have to understand where he came from," she said. "In Greece, growing up, your dad was poor. To survive he had to sneak over to other farms and steal figs to eat."

My mother went on to tell me how my dad's dad, my grandfather, spent all his days in the coffee shop, drinking strong Greek coffee, playing cards, and providing little for the family.

"Your father purposed in his heart that when he had a family of his own, he would never fail to provide for his children," my mom explained. "Providing food and money for us is how he shows his love."

That talk with my mom helped me so much. I understood my dad so much better and could see with new eyes how he cared. I felt more tender toward him from that day on.

The minute you understand how someone needs love and how he or she shows it, you won't fight your relationship with him or her anymore. You'll be able to put yourself in his or her shoes, and you'll grow in your relationship.

You may not have come from a broken home, but maybe your spouse did. Maybe you can't understand what it feels like to watch a home break up because of unfaithfulness. But you can't just look at your spouse and say, "What's wrong with you? Get over it. Don't you trust me?" That's not being tender hearted.

Beloved, I want you to heal your soul and make progress in your relationships.

Can you imagine Jacob all his life wondering, "Why does my dad love Esau more than me?"

The Bible tells us why:

> *Now Isaac loved [and favored] Esau, because he enjoyed eating his game…*
>
> *Genesis 25:28 AMP*

I wonder if Jacob understood why his father felt closer to Esau. Did he know that Isaac's dad, Abraham (Jacob's grandfather), also had a son who was a hunter, Ishmael? (Genesis 21:20 NKJV)

We're told Abraham loved Ishmael. You can read the whole story in Genesis 17 through 22. It says that Abraham loved Ishmael so much that at one point he prayed to God and said, "Let him be the one who is the chosen heir." (Genesis 17:18) Did Isaac see the close relationship between his father, Abraham, and his brother, Ishmael, and somehow connect hunting with love?

In fact, think about Isaac's life as a teenage boy. You're probably familiar with the story of how Abraham heard from God and took Isaac, the younger son (not the hunter, Ishmael), up to Mount Moriah to sacrifice him. Imagine being Isaac as a young man, being bound up and lying on an altar. I don't care how holy you are, when you see daddy standing over you with a knife trying to kill you, you're going to have a lot to process emotionally down the road!

Is it any wonder then if, in Isaac's soul somewhere deep down, Esau's being a hunter meant so much to him? Could it have possibly been because Ishmael meant so much to his father, Abraham? We can only speculate on that based on what we read in the Scripture, but I think it's clear that Isaac and Esau were more emotionally connected.

For us today, we must realize that we would make so much progress in our relationships if we truly tried to understand what people were walking through.

Tender love brings people together. It's easy to become judgmental and condemning when you've never battled what another is facing. But tender love says, "I don't know what that's like, but I'm just going to keep loving you and try to understand."

Love is being tender hearted. It's being exclusive, inclusive, and it's even more.

There's also a fourth aspect of the pillar of godly love that we must understand.

TOUGH LOVE

There will be times, to be sure, when God will direct you to show tough love to someone in your life. If a friend's decisions are sidetracking or destroying their relationships, you need to be willing to speak the truth at all costs.

Tough love puts the future on the line.

I think that's why Simon Cowell's tell-it-like-it-is honesty on the TV show *American Idol* years ago was appreciated by so many. As one of the judges, he didn't hesitate to tell a contestant, "You can't sing. Get off the stage." Most of his comments were probably over the top on purpose, but I'm guessing many were beneficial. The momentary pain from his stinging comments kept many people from chasing an unattainable dream, perhaps for years.

> *Truth is willing to risk the momentary feelings for the future relationship.*

Thankfully, my wife's occasional tough love toward me is much nicer than Simon Cowell's version. One issue Jackie and I worked through early in our marriage involved money, specifically my reaction to her spending it. Pretty much any of it.

Because of my upbringing, I wanted to save, save, save... and save some more. When she went to the grocery store and spent, say, $125 instead of the $100 I thought was sufficient, let's just say I didn't react very well. Of course, I didn't yell or anything like that, but I did make my displeasure evident.

My attitude began to weigh on Jackie, and she came to me one day and asked if we could talk. She calmly said, "What you're doing bothers me. I'm very careful with our money, and your attitude is affecting my heart toward you."

Jackie didn't make any demands. She didn't say she was leaving me, and she wasn't mean about it. She was confronting me from a position of love, and I had to work through it. I wasn't excited to hear what she was saying, but any hurt feelings in the short-term were so worth it as we figured out better ways to handle and talk about our finances for the future.

> *No discipline seems pleasant at the time, but painful. Later on, however, it produces a harvest of righteousness and peace for those who have been trained by it.*
>
> *Hebrews 12:11 NIV*

Tough love hurts sometimes. When you show tough love to your children, for example, it's painful—for them and for you. But if there are sin issues in their lives, for the sake of your home and your kids' future families and homes, those issues cannot be ignored. They must be brought into the light in a loving, firm way.

If you recall, godly wisdom anticipates the future and sees the reaping before the sowing. Tough love is also forwarding-looking. Truth is willing to risk the momentary feelings for the future relationship.

SACRIFICIAL LOVE

The fifth and final aspect of love that we need to build strong lives and homes is sacrificial love.

Sacrificial love says, "You come first. I come last."

This type of love is giving. It doesn't make demands. It is the exact opposite of how we see Rachel behaving toward Jacob a few years into their marriage:

> *When Rachel saw that she bore Jacob no children, Rachel envied her sister, and said to Jacob, "Give me children, or else I die!"*
>
> *Genesis 30:1 NKJV*

That's not a very good example of sacrificial love, is it?

Sacrificial love is the foundation of Christianity. When Jesus was on Earth, He made it clear that He did not come to be served but to serve and to give His life as a ransom for many (Matthew 20:28).

There are two key principles I want you to see about sacrificial love:

1. **Sacrificial love will cost you your life's resources**. When Christ willingly died on the cross, it was the most incredible act of love the world will ever see. If we truly fathom the sacrifice He made

for us, we can't help but respond. That's what real sacrificial love does.

Greater love has no one than this: to lay down one's life for one's friends.

John 15:13 NIV

If we follow Christ's example, our sacrificial love will come with a cost. It will cost us time—an afternoon of playing soccer with our kids rather than enjoying our own hobbies. It will cost us money—buying lunch for a friend who is trying to sort through some challenges. For our troops who serve our country sacrificially, it costs their personal comfort, time with their families, and for some, sacrificial love costs their very breath.

2. **Sacrificial love gives and never gives out**. I'm sure you have heard the saying, "Go the extra mile." Did you know it comes from a teaching from Jesus?

And whoever compels you to go one mile, go with him two.

Matthew 5:41 NIV

In Israel during the reign of the Romans, if a soldier walked by a Jewish man working his field, the soldier could rightfully say, "You have to carry my pack for a mile," and the man would have to comply.

Jesus was telling us, yes, go that first mile. It's your responsibility. Do your part. But the second mile is not your responsibility. Nevertheless, at Mile Two, we should tell our friend (spouse, child, or parent, etc.), "You're tired and overwhelmed. Let me carry your pack, your burden, for one more mile."

Sacrificial love says, "I'm willing to give up my life's resources for you. Whatever you need it's yours." That kind of love also says, "I'm willing to do my part, and I'm willing to do your part, too."

Just think what this kind of love will do to that person's mind and heart!

There's no love without sacrifice. There's no love without laying down your life and putting yourself last.

Like integrity and loyalty, the pillar of love is never contingent on what we get back from others.

When we put all five aspects of God's love into our lives and our relationships, our hearts will become strong and unshakeable through the storms of life.

PILLAR 5
ACCOUNTABILITY

ACCOUNTABILITY

THE PILLAR OF SPIRITUAL HEALTH

Of all the chapters in this book, this will be the one people will be tempted to skip. I hope I'm wrong, but I can't fight human nature.

I've lived long enough to know that people tend to scatter when they hear the word accountability.

There are two reasons people get uncomfortable about this topic:

1. They want to hide something in their lives that is unhealthy and/or embarrassing; or

2. They think they have no need for accountability. "Who, me? I don't have any issues in my life—at least none I can't manage myself. But my sister-in-law? She sure could use some help!"

You're still reading, though, so you must understand or sense the tremendous value of accountability. Or, you're simply curious about it. Either way, I encourage you to continue on with our study because accountability is a vital pillar of a strong Christian life.

Here's how I would define this important pillar for strong spiritual health: **Accountability is your willingness for your heart to be examined.**

It is built on prayers like this one by King David in the Bible:

Search me, O God, and know my heart; try me, and know my anxieties; and see if there is any wicked way in me; and lead me in the way everlasting.

Psalm 139:23–24 NKJV

If you're on God's path now, following Him closely, accountability will keep you spiritually healthy. And if something is wrong inside, accountability will help you get healthy so that you can live a long and prosperous life.

I understand why a person might be reluctant to have his or her heart searched. Submitting yourself to an examination can leave you feeling vulnerable and uneasy. I know I wasn't looking forward to my latest "you've turned-a-new-decade" medical check-up. But for the sake of our health, physical and spiritual, and our futures, we shouldn't put off our "exams."

> *Allowing others to help us be whole and healed is the meaning of accountability.*

Many of us would rather try to manage the unhealthy issues in our lives. We think we can manage our anger on our own. We try to manage our envy and jealousy. We try to manage our alcohol or food consumption. You name it. But at the end of the day, if we don't deal with our problem areas and if we don't acknowledge our struggles and sin, they will eventually get the best of us.

A few years back, a pregnant woman from our church started having a pain in her side. At first, she hoped it would go away, or if it didn't, that she could just endure the pain. But out of concern for the little one inside her, she went to the doctor and had everything checked it out. Tests revealed a tumor in her kidney.

Your health is no small matter, physical or spiritual. It's nothing to play with. Imagine what could have happened if that young mother had tried to deal with the pain herself? No, she needed to be healed. And, thank God, the doctors were able to remove the tumor. Today she and her child are whole and healthy.

Friend, allowing others to help us be whole and healed is the meaning of accountability.

Every good tree bears good fruit, but a bad tree bears bad fruit.

Matthew 7:17 NKJV

Our spiritual health determines our fruit. And one day each of us will stand before the Lord. How terrible it will be if He says, "I had this great plan for you. You were supposed to do this and that—to produce good fruit and make a great impact on your family and your community. Why didn't you?"

GET FACE TO FACE

We will all face God after we leave this Earth. Until then, we can try to avoid Him—try our best to hide or ignore the sin in our lives and the things that are just plain harmful. But, one way or another, He will bring about a situation to get our attention and to seek help. He doesn't do this to be mean. He does this out of love. He is telling us, "I just can't leave you in this unhealthy state. I want to see you grow strong and be productive in your home, at work, and in your walk with me."

In Jacob's case, God used a barrier, of sorts, to get his attention and to bring about a new life. It all started after Laban finally caught up to Jacob's caravan when Jacob was fleeing with his family to Canaan. Rachel and Leah's father was none too happy:

> Then Laban said to Jacob: "What have you done? You've deceived me, and you've carried off my daughters like captives in war. Why did you run off secretly and deceive me? Why didn't you tell me, so I could send you away with joy and singing to the music of timbrels and harps? You didn't even let me kiss my grandchildren and my daughters goodbye. You have done a foolish thing."
>
> Genesis 31:26–28 NIV

The men argued for a time, questioning each other's motives and actions, until they agreed they needed a covenant between them— something to keep them accountable. It's interesting to note that they set up a *literal pillar* to symbolize their agreement.

> Laban ... said to Jacob, "Here is this… pillar I have set up between you and me. [The] pillar is a witness, that I will not go past this heap to your side to harm you and that you will not go past this pillar to my side to harm me. May God… judge between us."
>
> Genesis 31:51–53 NIV

If Jacob was at all tempted to stay with Laban, in his familiar home of twenty years, God had made sure that wasn't going to happen. It's as if

God was saying, "You can't go back, Jacob. Move forward, and go to your ancestral land."

But this was only one part of God's plan. Jacob soon realized it wouldn't be easy to go forward. An angry twin brother lay in wait ahead. Esau had previously vowed to kill Jacob.

> *Esau held a grudge against Jacob because of the blessing his father had given him. He said to himself, "The days of mourning for my father are near; then I will kill my brother Jacob."*
>
> *Genesis 27:41 NIV*

To make peace, Jacob sent messengers ahead to tell Esau that Jacob was on his way and had cattle, donkeys, other livestock, and servants as gifts for Esau. The messengers returned with seemingly threatening news:

> *...We went to your brother Esau, and now he is coming to meet you, and four hundred men are with him.*
>
> *Genesis 32:6 NIV*

The thought of coming against all those men filled Jacob with fear and distress.

Because of his covenant with Laban, Jacob couldn't go backward, and he couldn't go forward. He was hemmed in. It was a real-life Psalm 139:5 moment: "You hem me in behind and before, and you lay your hand upon me" (NIV).

It was as if God was saying, "Jacob, it's time for you to make changes in your life, once and for all. I want you to be fruitful and to fulfill the purpose I have for you."

For you and me, too, if we're not willing to be accountable and live on God's terms, He will hem us in. He will use situations that bring us to a place where we're desperate to be whole and healthy— even situations we've brought upon ourselves. He uses these tight places in life to bring us face to face with Him to help us grow into all that He has for us.

Why would God allow you to go through tough times? Because you'll discover Him in your struggles and in the places where you feel hemmed in or constrained in ways you might never discover Him if there were only blessings in front of you.

If God somehow magically took care of everything around you all the time, you wouldn't need to trust Him for anything. You wouldn't need faith, and you wouldn't grow spiritually strong.

I am reminded of an old episode of *The Andy Griffith Show*. (Don't you love good old-fashioned television?) Andy's son, Opie, was facing a tough situation—a bully was demanding his milk money every day before school. Afraid of the bully's threats to give him a "knuckle sandwich" Opie kept on handing over his nickels day after day. At first, Andy wanted to intervene, but then he saw the wisdom of letting Opie fight his own battles.

The next day, on Opie's way to school, he turned a corner and practically ran into the bully. "Where's my nickel, boy?"

The next time the viewers see Opie, he is walking into his dad's courthouse with the biggest shiner you could imagine. He points to his black eye and proudly asks Andy, "Ain't she a beaut, Pa?" Opie had defeated the bully.

Of course, if Andy had stepped in and solved his son's problem for him, Opie never would have experienced the victory he did (painful as it was). I know it's only a television show, but can't you see parallels to real life in it?

The enemy of our souls wants to bully you. But God wants you to grow strong to defeat that thief. God doesn't want you forking over your "milk money"—the things He's blessed you with.

God doesn't want you to lose. He wants you to gain and have a strong life, home, and family. He wants to give you His strength when you cry out to Him.

Jacob's response to his desperate situation was to call out to God.

> *Save me, I pray, from the hand of my brother Esau, for I am afraid he will come and attack me, and also the mothers with their children.*
>
> *Genesis 32:11 NIV*

That night, Jacob took his plea to a whole new level. He actually wrestled God and demanded a blessing! It all started when Jacob sent his family and servants to a safer place. Alone in the wilderness, Jacob was awakened in the night by a mysterious being. (Many scholars believe this was God Himself.) And the two began to wrestle.

> *Jacob replied, "I will not let you go unless you bless me."*

The man asked him, "What is your name?"

"Jacob," he answered.

Then the man said, "Your name will no longer be Jacob, but Israel, because you have struggled with God and with humans and have overcome." …Then he blessed him there.

Genesis 32:26–29 NIV

So Jacob called the name of the place Peniel [which means "face of God"]: "For I have seen God face to face, and my life is preserved."

Genesis 32:30 NKJV [Author's Note]

What a privilege, to see God face to face. You and I likely won't see God in the same manner as Jacob. Still, we should seek our Heavenly Father's face in prayer.

But we all, with unveiled face, beholding as in a mirror the glory of the Lord, are being transformed into the same image from glory to glory, just as by the Spirit of the Lord.

2 Corinthians 3:18 NKJV

Here's the beautiful thing about God: **He doesn't bring us face to face with Him for the purpose of intimidating us. He does it to inspire us.**

As we see God and all His goodness, it inspires us to want to change. We can bring all our faults and weaknesses to Him. There is transformative power when we hold up our lives to God's holy mirror. He will not condemn us. He will lovingly reveal His desires for us to grow strong:

"I don't want your anger to get the best of you."

"I don't want depression to get the best of you."

"I don't want your insecurities to motivate you anymore."

"I don't want your addictions to get the best of you."

What is God telling you as you seek His face?

DON'T RUN FROM ACCOUNTABILITY

Jacob could have run from God, but he didn't. He stayed even though it was uncomfortable. He refused to let go until God had changed him and blessed him.

I urge you, don't run when God reveals an issue in your heart. Instead, get to a place where you yield to Him and cry out, "God, change me! I'm tired of living like this!"

I love the following blessing that Paul prayed over the church at Thessalonica. I encourage you to pray it over yourself and your family.

> *God doesn't want to embarrass us. He wants to empower us.*

> *Now may the God of peace Himself sanctify you completely; and may your whole spirit, soul, and body be preserved blameless at the coming of our Lord Jesus Christ.*
>
> *1 Thessalonians 5:23 NKJV*

God's desire is for you to become accountable to Him and to the people He has put in your life so that you can become completely whole.

I am convinced Jesus died a complete death to bring about our complete healing, but one thing that scares people away from seeking accountability is the desire for privacy. Let me assure you, God is not interested in exposing your struggles to the world. He wants to deal with you on the inside.

It seems like a small detail, but God didn't wrestle with Jacob until he was alone. **God doesn't want to embarrass us. He wants to empower us.**

The enemy, on the other hand, attacks people in hopes of maximum fallout. He wants us to live with our issues and shortcomings, and he wants us to take down others when we fall. He wants our anger to cause us to lose our jobs and our spouses; our addictions to cause car wrecks; our weaknesses to destroy relationships. He loves it when ministers live in sin and put a blot on the name of Christianity.

But that's not God's way. Before someone's struggles ever made the headlines, I can assure you that God was quietly working on that person's heart, wanting them to yield to His healing. He might start by shining a penlight on the issue, saying, "Let's talk about this." If the person tells God "no" and doesn't deal with the problem, it grows bigger and becomes harder and harder to keep private. Eventually, the penlight becomes a flashlight and then a spotlight, until the person ultimately rejects God's nudging, and everybody finds out about their unhealthy ways.

> *Whether our default reactions are sinful or just plain harmful, they cause us to be unfruitful.*

When you refuse to allow the Lord's correction, you trap yourself in your struggles and open your life up to sorrow and shame.

ACCOUNTABILITY RESETS OUR DEFAULT REACTIONS

We all have default reactions to certain situations. If we feel backed into a corner, some of us default to telling a lie. When we get disappointed, some of us quit. When we get frustrated, we often get angry. If our expectations aren't met, we pull away and disengage our hearts. When I was younger and someone said something against me, I really had to work at not responding with bad language.

Whether our default reactions are sinful or just plain harmful, they cause us to be unfruitful. They also cause us to back away from accountability, which is the very thing we need to become spiritually healthy so we can be fruitful and productive.

As I mentioned, at any point, Jacob could have run away from his troubles—his unwanted marriage to Leah, his deceptive father-in-law, his lack of livestock. But he didn't. Even when he was wrestling God, Jacob wouldn't let go!

> *So He said to him, "What is your name?" He said, "Jacob."*
>
> *Genesis 2:27 NKJV*

In many cultures, both ancient and modern, people take great stock in the meaning of a person's name, much more than how it sounds. In the Bible, God re-named several people, giving them a new identities and new ways to act and react to the world.

» Abram became Abraham *(father of many nations)*.

» Simon became Peter *(the rock)*.

» Solomon was also known as Jedidiah *(loved by the Lord)*.

» Jacob became Israel *(the one who struggled with God and humans and overcame)*.

Before Jacob wrestled with God, whenever he declared who he was, he was saying, "My name is Jacob. I'm the second born. I'm insecure. And my insecurities are making me feel like I have to fight for everything that I get. I'm tired of fighting. I'm tired of manipulating situations. I'm tired of always feeling like everything depends on me to get ahead."

Whether Jacob was with his brother or his dad or with Laban, there was a part of his insecurity that brought up this default reaction in him to fight and scrap for whatever he needed. The feeling that everything depended on him making things happen for himself was Jacob's default reaction because he was second born.

But when Jacob wrestled with God, God changed his name to Israel. He didn't just give him a new name, though. God did something even deeper in Jacob:

> This is what the Lord says—he who created you, Jacob, he who formed you, Israel: "Do not fear, for I have redeemed you; I have summoned you by name; you are mine."
>
> Isaiah 43:1 NIV

"Do not fear," God told Israel (Jacob). No longer did the heel-grabber, the second born, have to react to life from a fearful, insecure place. God had redeemed him.

You and I don't need to change our names, but we should consider how we react to God's loving correction and desire for our accountability. We shouldn't be afraid of having our hearts examined. We should run to God with our weaknesses so that He can help us turn them into strengths.

God is waiting for us to come to Him to be healed and made whole.

SUBMIT TO A SPIRITUAL AUDIT

For all the negative connotations related to the Internal Revenue Service (the IRS), their ability to audit tax returns undoubtedly encourages people to be more honest and use the utmost care when they file their taxes. The thought of being audited by the IRS can evoke an awful feeling of dread, but passing an audit with flying colors can be exhilarating. I know people who have been given greater tax refunds after an audit! That's the reward of keeping good books.

I am so glad I'm married to a woman who is very detailed and keeps fantastic records for our household. Accountability for our expenses would be difficult without Jackie. She is my accountability partner.

Do you have an accountability partner? And I'm not referring to your business and personal mileage. I'm talking about someone you can go to in order to keep yourself honest.

> *Two are better than one, Because they have a good reward for their labor.*
>
> *Ecclesiastes 4:9 NKJV*

God never wanted us to do life alone. For this reason, church, small groups, prayer partners, and mentors are essential to us being accountable. Do you have an accountability partner in life? If you do, you can give an answer with a clear conscience that your records, whereabouts, and actions are all accurate, aboveboard, and pure. This is the secret to passing what I like to call a "spiritual audit."

Using the acronym "IRS," here are the three basic elements to building greater accountability into your life:

» **I—Identify a mentor**. Is there a trustworthy voice in your life who is speaking to you? It's great to have time with God, but we also need people to guide us, especially mature believers, as mentors. We need to put ourselves in places where we allow leaders to deal with us privately or in a small group setting— someone we can walk up to and say, "Can you help me? I'm really struggling with this." We need mentors to help us move on to spiritual growth.

» **R—Reveal your struggle**. Sin grows in the dark. Don't try to hide your struggles and sins. Let God's healing light into your life by seeking out a safe place to work them out with mentors and leaders who have overcome what you are facing and have victory. The enemy wants you to hide your head in shame, but God wants you to be completely set free. James 5:16 tells us, "Confess your faults to one another, and pray one for another, that you may be healed" (KJV).

» **S—Submit to counsel.** When a trustworthy person does speak into your life, listen to him or her and take action. As we confess our faults to one another, we will be healed, but healing is a process. We must be willing to hear and accept wisdom from a mentor or counselor and follow it consistently. It's the power of acting on the Word of God that brings about real and lasting life change.

ACCOUNTABILITY CHANGES OUR WALK

I believe with all my heart that God wants us to embrace a life of accountability and spiritual health to gain freedom from the things that have held us back.

When Jacob wrestled with God, he refused to let go of his divine visitor. He refused to leave the encounter until he received God's blessing on his life—and he got it.

> *...Thy name shall be called no more Jacob, but Israel: for as a prince hast thou power with God and with men, and hast prevailed.*
>
> *Genesis 32:28 KJV*

God said to him, "You're no longer Jacob. You're Israel—the prince. You're not second. You're first. It doesn't matter how the world sees you. It only matters how I see you."

Then God touched Jacob's hip. And when Jacob got up he left the encounter with a limp. Now to some, this part of the story may seem confusing, but I believe it's an outward picture of how Jacob's inward life was changed.

Beloved, sometimes in life, situations that hemmed us in can hurt us. They can cause permanent damage. Jacob limped the rest of his life physically—but not on the inside. From that day on he didn't limp through life. He was the prince of God's people, and his struggle with insecurity was gone. I've said it before, but it bears repeating: Jacob may have been second born, but he finished first in life.

Some time ago, I received the following letter that is a powerful testament to how God works. I've shortened it, and I have changed a few details for privacy reasons, but as the letter-writer noted, I pray it helps you somehow.

Dear Pastor Steve and Jackie,

I'm not really sure where to start this letter. I am currently in jail. This is my first and hopefully only time here. Most people say they wish they had never come, and they count down the days until they get out. I can't say that. I need to be here. I've put my faith in God here, and He's given me peace.

You see, I can't trust myself, and I've been lost now for quite some time trying to find my way. I'm an addict, and, yes, it was my addiction that led me to where I am. I've tried over and over again to live a sober life. I've succeeded for periods of time only to build a life and watch it crumble around me. I've been sitting here trying to figure out exactly where I've been going wrong.

I'm pretty sure I've figured it out. You see, until recently I hadn't accepted the Lord as my Savior and lived for Him. But that is exactly what I am doing now. I attended your church with my parents a few times. I feel like I have failed my family over and over and over. But the time has come for me to live and give myself one hundred percent to God.

My father tells me, "Read the Bible; see yourself in the Bible." That's what I've been doing, and I have found God in a way I would have never found Him if I hadn't come here.

I'm writing you in the hope that God can use my story to help someone else in some way.

Friend, I believe with all my heart that when God hems you in to a position of accountability, it's for your growth.

Some of you may have wounds from situations you brought on yourself, but God can redeem them.

Maybe, like the woman in the letter, you committed a crime and served time in prison for it. You have a criminal record, but God is redeeming you and healing you of your past. It may seem as if you have an impediment in the natural, but God has healed you on the inside. Maybe you've suffered from an addiction. You've lost precious relationships, or you feel as if years of your life have been wasted. No, you can't turn back time, but God wants to bring you complete freedom today so that you can walk on with Him in victory in the future.

God, let us establish the pillar of accountability in our lives and our homes. Let us be accountable to one another and lift each other up without condemnation. Help us to be healed and to restore and empower those who are struggling so that we can all be healthy and whole—not just for ourselves, but for the generations to come—in Jesus' name. Amen.

PILLAR 6

RIGHTEOUSNESS

RIGHTEOUSNESS

CHOOSE TO BELIEVE AND OBEY

Every day, you and I face hundreds of decisions, if not more. Most are on the small side: *Can I get away with hitting the snooze button again? Should I take the expressway to work or the back roads? After dinner, should we watch a movie or play a game?* And of course, life is filled with plenty of big decisions, too. *What college should I go to? How many children do we want? Can I really trust God?*

The thing is, we know both big and even seemingly small decisions can have an impact on us and our families. Sometimes we get paralyzed by all the choices we have, and we live in fear, worrying about each and every possible option. Some decisions may be difficult to make, and we avoid them altogether until we're backed into a corner and have no other choice. But to build strong lives and homes, we must learn how to make tough decisions. Our decisions in life must be based on God's way of doing things.

The two biggest decisions a person can make are to believe in God and to obey Him. Obviously, these aren't one-time choices. Each day, we must keep believing Him and obeying Him in whatever situations come our way.

RIGHTEOUSNESS MAKES THE DECISION TO BELIEVE AND OBEY

Together believing and obeying lead us to righteousness—God's right way of doing things. The pillar of righteousness has two sides.

The first part of righteousness requires believing God. Look at what the writer of the book of Romans, whom most scholars believe to be Paul, said about Abraham's faith.

And because of Abraham's faith, God counted him as righteous.

Romans 4:22 NLT

Abraham's believing God was accounted to him as righteousness. But it doesn't stop there. The pillar of righteousness is two sided.

Righteousness not only believes God. Righteousness obeys God. The New Testament writer James, wrote this about Abraham's righteousness:

Was not Abraham our father justified by works when he offered Isaac his son on the altar? Do you see that faith was working together with his works, and by works faith was made perfect? And the Scripture was fulfilled which says, "Abraham believed God, and it was accounted to him for righteousness."

James 2:21–23 NKJV

So, here we are. Two New Testament writers seem to differ in how they explain righteousness. Paul says righteousness is believing, while James says righteousness (justification) is obeying. Which one is it? Paul says "believe" and James says "obey." Do they contradict each other? No. The answer is not either/or. It's both/and.

Obedience doesn't contradict our righteousness. It complements it. Believing and obeying merge, and they become one. A righteous person says, "Because we believe God, we are going to obey God." Every individual and every home should have that philosophy.

The key is to first believe. If you try to obey before you believe, whatever "right" things you attempt will not be His righteousness. They'll be done out of your own sense of righteousness, which is really just self-righteousness.

Have you ever seen holier-than-thou, religious, self-righteous people who, because they "perform," think they are right with God? That's not how you get right with God. We are right with God not because of what *WE do*, but because of what *HE did*. And what He did should so move our hearts that we will make the decision to live for Him and obey Him.

First John 3:7 says: "He that doeth righteousness is righteous, even as he is righteous" (KJV). Here is my translation. I call it the "PSV"—the "Pastor

Steve Version"—of that Scripture: **He who makes the tough decision to believe, makes the tough decision to obey.**

Righteousness is saying, "I'm going to make the tough decision to obey because I believe that's what God wants me to do."

JACOB'S RIGHTEOUS DECISION

When Jacob was renamed Israel by the Lord, it foreshadowed the fact that his twelve sons would later make up the twelve tribes of the nation of Israel. There was tension among the boys, though, because Jacob favored Joseph, Rachel's firstborn son. And when Rachel later died giving birth to Benjamin, it only intensified Jacob's affection for Joseph and Benjamin over his other sons.

> *Righteousness not only believes God. Righteousness obeys God.*

In one of the most well-known Bible stories of all time, we are told that Joseph went out to the field with ten of his brothers, and they jumped him. They threw him into a pit and sold him to Ishmaelite traders who took him to Egypt.

Afterward, the brothers took Joseph's coat, covered it with goat's blood, and returned home. When Jacob saw the bloody coat, the sons didn't even have to make up a story. It was Jacob who jumped to the conclusion that wild animals must have attacked Joseph and dragged him off. Jacob's grief was intense. Genesis 37:35 says he refused to be comforted.

More than a decade later, Jacob's land was suffering from famine, and he sent the ten brothers to Egypt to buy food. If you know Joseph's story, (the full account can be read in Genesis 37–50), you know that not only was Joseph still alive, but also he had become Egypt's second in command, just below Pharaoh. When his brothers arrived, Joseph knew who they were immediately, but they did not recognize Joseph. Joseph began to test them with questions.

"Are these all your brothers?"

"No, we have one more. His name is Benjamin. He's our father's favorite, and he's back home."

"Oh, you have a father? Is he alive?"

"Yes, his name is Jacob, and he's alive."

After some back and forth, Joseph ended with this: "Here's some grain, but don't come back for more unless you bring your brother Benjamin."

When the ten reported back to their father, Jacob was torn. He was faced with a decision that seemed impossible to make. He reasoned, "Should I let Benjamin go, or not? Rachel is dead. Joseph is dead. Benjamin is the only thing of her I have left. If I lose him, I'll be devastated!"

Jacob was obviously pained by the dilemma. God had brought him to a place where he was going to have to make a tough decision.

DECIDING BECOMES TOUGH WHEN IT AFFECTS US PERSONALLY

You know, it's easy to tell someone else what to do in a hard situation if the outcome doesn't affect us personally. When someone we care for wants input on a decision, yes, we can help them carefully weigh out the options, but at the end of the day, each of us needs to make our own decisions, because we will be the ones who will personally walk out the consequences.

No one is immune from facing hard choices in life.

Jacob was in agony thinking about the possibility of losing Benjamin, Rachel's only other son. Jacob had to decide whether he was going to trust God with Benjamin's life or not.

No one is immune to facing hard choices in life. You know deciding to take a stand for Christ is the right thing to do, for example, but it may cost you some friends. Tough decisions may be required at your work, even though it may make you unpopular.

As you seek God's righteousness in your life, be prepared to wrestle with four common dilemmas related to making righteous decisions.

DILEMMA 1: WHAT WE BELIEVE AFFECTS HOW WE DECIDE

God's Truth vs. My Truth

There is God's truth, and there is our own sense of truth. Which truth do you think we should believe and trust?

Maybe God is asking you to forgive someone in your life. Your own sense of truth will make you think: *How can I ever forgive the man who abused me? Why should he get away with what he did, while I deal with it for the rest of my life?* That may be your truth, but God's truth says if you walk in forgiveness, God will heal you. You won't be imprisoned by the pain from that abuse, and you'll be able to live a life free of bitterness.

God's truth and the world's truth are usually going to be diametrically opposed to each other. If you are a husband, God's truth says, "I want you to love your wife, give her your all, and serve her." But your truth might react: *If I do that, I'll be taking out the trash and drawing bubble baths all the time. No way!*

God's truth doesn't accommodate our limited viewpoints. It says, "You need to lay your life down for her in the same way that I laid down My life for you." This is the real truth—the secret to having a great marriage. If you're a wife, God's truth says, "I want you to submit to your husband." But your own mind may tell you, *If I submit to my husband, he's going to walk all over me.* Don't believe it. Your "truth" is really a lie. Submit to your husband, because God's truth says something dynamic will take place in your marriage when you do.

God's truth is always right and righteous, but our truth is only "a way that seems right, but its end is the way of death" (Proverbs 14:12 NKJV). Which truth will you believe?

What you believe affects how you decide. If you believe life should be self-gratifying, you'll make every decision based on satisfying yourself. If you believe you should lay your life down for God, for your neighbors, and for your family, you'll make all your decisions based on that.

> *God, please give us the right perspective to make righteous decisions. Amen.*

DILEMMA 2: EVERY DECISION HAS A COST

We must choose which price to pay.

Someone once said there are two pains to choose from: The pain of the moment, or the pain of regret. We must choose which one we want to pay.

Jacob had to decide, "If I send Benjamin to Egypt with my other sons to get food, I could lose him. But if I don't send him, our whole nation will starve." Both decisions had a cost. Thankfully, Jacob made the right decision and let Benjamin go.

The most rewarding seasons of my life have come when I made a tough decision because it was the right thing to do. It seems as if every time I've come to a barrier in life, there is a tough decision to be made to get past it. Sometimes I'll just pray, "Oh, God! Do something!" In effect, I want God to make the decision for me. But God usually answers me. "I'm waiting on you. You choose!" And sure enough, when I finally make the tough choice, somehow, the barrier is broken, and I come out blessed on the other side.

If you want to break the limits holding you down at work, make that tough decision and show them who you are and what you can do. If you want to take your marriage to another level, if you want to take your walk with God to another level, if you want to take your business to another level, if you want to walk in victory as you've never walked before, if you want to take your church to another level, make the tough decision that's in front of you. Every breakthrough in life comes from making a hard decision. That's how it works.

God, give us the strength to make hard choices and the strength to live them out. Amen.

DILEMMA 3: DECISIONS ARE MADE IN THE SPIRIT OF COURAGE OR COMFORT

Sometimes the right decisions don't seem to make sense.

Your decisions in life will either be made in the spirit of courage or in the spirit of comfort. I remember when my dad was about to move away from our area. We were eating at a Waffle House restaurant when he said, "Son, move with me to North Carolina." I was going to Bible college at the time, and I didn't want to move. In reality, I had my eye on this brunette there, and I wanted to stay for her. (College was a front!) It was a tough decision, though, because I wouldn't have a place to stay after Dad moved. I would be forced to sleep in my 1978 Chevrolet Monte Carlo. It was silver with a crushed-red-velvet interior and a headliner that was sagging because the sunroof leaked. I couldn't afford an apartment.

I can't recall my exact words, but I took the time to pray: "God, I want what You have for me. I know my destiny is here in this city with this woman named Jackie. I'm making a tough decision to stay here. Please help me."

I am so thankful God helped me make a courageous decision rather than a comfortable one.

Sometimes tough decisions for God don't make sense, but you have to make them because they are a step of faith. Jacob had to trust that God would protect Benjamin in Egypt. It would have brought comfort to have Benjamin at home, but Jacob showed his faith in allowing Benjamin to travel. God asks us to do the illogical at times. **If we will obey Him in the illogical, God will do the impossible.**

It's not always easy to find the courage to do what's right. In certain situations, you might hope that someone else steps up in faith. You hope that some other Christian in the neighborhood decides to reach out to the woman down the street who needs God but is hard to be around sometimes.

More than five hundred years before Christ lived on Earth, four lepers showed great courage when they stepped out in faith during another famine. You can read their story in 2 Kings 7, but I'll share highlights here.

As the famine dragged on, the four lepers suffered more and more. The handouts they received while begging outside the city gate were no longer sufficient. They couldn't travel to a new place, because an enemy army was camped nearby. The lepers were hemmed in. They had no logical options. "If we stay here, we will die," one of the lepers told his friends. "But if we go out where the enemy is, we will die. What should we do?"

"Well, we've got nothing to lose," another leper replied. "Let's go out there. Maybe something will happen." It seemed illogical, but they did it. And when they arrived at the enemy's camp, instead of being killed or taken prisoner, they found it empty—empty of people, that is. The Lord had scared away the army beforehand, but the soldiers' belongings remained— all their silver, their gold, and their huge supply of food! As the lepers ate their fill, they realized they should share their abundance with the people in the city who were starving.

When I think about those lepers, this thought comes to me: **Other people lived off of their courage.**

I don't know about you, but I don't want to live off of someone else's courage. I want to step out by faith. I want to be willing to forgive. I want to be willing to lay down my life for the Lord.

Lord, whatever You're calling us to do, let us decide
to obey You in the spirit of courage. Amen.

DILEMMA 4: INDECISIVENESS KILLS

Don't put off or play down decisions.

Indecisiveness kills. Just ask the squirrel. He gets in the middle of the street, and what does he do? The spirit of indecisiveness comes on him. "Where do I go? Do I go back? Do I go forward?" And if the squirrel remains indecisive, guess what happens? Splat!

We cannot put things off when a decision is needed now.

> *And it came to pass, when they had eaten up the grain… their father said to them, "Go back, buy us a little food."*
>
> Genesis 43:2 NKJV

Jacob put off the tough choice until he was out of options. He waited until they were out of grain. And then he told his sons to go buy "a *little* food." Are you kidding me? There were thousands of starving people in Canaan! His family could have been feasting with Joseph off the blessings of Egypt so much sooner, if only Jacob hadn't waited to release Benjamin to go.

Friends, don't put off making tough decisions, and don't downplay their importance, either. Your future is at stake. Your city and nation are at stake. Your family is at stake.

> **Today**, *if you will hear His voice,* **Do not harden your hearts**....
>
> Hebrews 3:15 NKJV [Author's Emphasis]

If you don't know Christ today, your soul is at stake. Please don't fool yourself into thinking, *I've got plenty of time to make Jesus Lord of my life.* You don't know that! No one knows what tomorrow will bring. Accept Christ as your Lord and Savior **today**! *(Friend, if you'd like to accept Christ as your Lord today, please hold your place here right now, and pray the prayer of salvation found in the end pages of this book. You can walk with Him in newness of life today.)*

When you put off making right decisions, it only gets harder and harder as time passes. A slow leak in your tire is more dangerous than a flat. A flat is inconvenient, but a slow leak makes you think you can keep going. That's what makes it dangerous. You'll be chugging along, getting by, when suddenly, you will experience a blowout.

God, may we walk in wisdom and make the decisions we need to make quickly. Amen.

RIGHTEOUS DECISIONS BRING FULLNESS

Of all the possible decisions you and I will make today, the two most courageous and life-giving ones are these: **to believe God** and **to obey Him**. When we believe and obey, He will bring fullness to our lives.

> *...I have set before you life and death, blessing and cursing: therefore choose life....*
>
> Deuteronomy 30:19 NKJV

> *If you are willing and obedient, you shall eat the good of the land.*
>
> Isaiah 1:19 NKJV

Let me tell you how this played out in Jacob's life. When Jacob's eleven sons finally arrived in Egypt, Joseph subjected them to more questioning until he finally caved to his emotions and announced, "I am Joseph, your brother, the one you beat and threw into a pit and sold as a slave." I'm sure their jaws dropped open, and they almost couldn't believe it.

The two most courageous and life-giving decisions we can make are to believe God and to obey Him.

When the brothers returned to Canaan, they stunned their father by saying, "Joseph is still alive! He's the ruler over all the land." The Bible says Jacob's "heart stood still" at the news (Genesis 45:26 NKJV). Not only had Benjamin returned to him unharmed, Jacob gained back the son he thought had died!

The enemy of our souls loves to sow seeds of defeat. He tells us if we make a courageous decision to stand up in the workplace, to make a choice at home to do the right thing, or to decide to raise our kids by God's righteous standard, we will somehow lose out. Something bad will happen. We will lose our own Benjamins. The truth is, **when you make a righteous decision, you'll not only see God do the impossible, you will see Him bring fullness into your life**.

Jacob was dumbfounded when both Benjamin and Joseph returned to his family. Never in a million years would Jacob have come up with the thought: *If I let Benjamin go, I'll get Joseph back.* But that's exactly what happened!

Ephesians 3:20 tells us, God "is able to do *exceedingly abundantly above all that we ask or think,* according to the power that works in us" (NKJV, Author's Emphasis). Jacob had the power within him, and you have the power within you to make right decisions. You have the power to say "yes" to Christ. You have the power to forgive. You have the power to make the courageous choice today that God has been asking you to make.

Boldly stand on the pillar of righteousness. Believe and obey. Say to yourself, "I've been waiting on God, but God has been waiting on me, and I'm just going to do it!"

SEE THE IMPOSSIBLE MADE POSSIBLE

There was a time when I wasn't enjoying life. I was working at the church seven days a week and hardly ever took a day off. I knew it wasn't healthy, but taking time off seemed impossible—there was just so much to do. But it finally got to the point where I knew something had to give.

"I have to stop working on Mondays," I told my wife one day. "We need a consistent day off—we need regular family nights and date nights." It wasn't long before my decision was confirmed. On our first Monday date night, Jackie and I were eating at Bonefish Grill, when she looked at me and asked, "How much life insurance do you have?"

What kind of crazy question was that for our first date night in months?

But Jackie was making a point: If I didn't stay committed to a better schedule, I probably wouldn't be around much longer. It scared me, but it also helped to confirm my need for balance in my life.

Now I love our date nights and family nights. They have brought us so much closer together as a couple and a family. I could have waited and wished for things to come together like that, but nothing would have happened. I had to make the right choice to make what seemed impossible come to pass, and in the end, the church and my life were both more blessed.

Time after time I've seen God bless His children who seek His righteousness in the decisions they make. I'll never forget how God worked in the life of a woman who had been addicted to pain pills for twenty years. My first conversation with her took place in my office, and my assistant was with us. The woman couldn't sit still, she was shaking so much from her addiction.

"God's got a better life for you than those pills offer," I told her. "What caused you to start using them?"

"When I was young, I had an abortion," she said. "Since then, I've been dulling the pain with pills."

I talked about how it was time for her to forgive herself, and my assistant and I said we would pray with her. As she continued to shake, I started by saying, "Just put your hands in mine, and let's pray that God will help you forgive yourself."

Before I could even continue, I felt her hands suddenly stop shaking. I knew God was flooding her life. After our time of prayer, she was already a different person. With conviction she told us, "I'm going to do everything I have to do. I'm not going to do these drugs anymore. God wants something better for me."

Today, I'm happy to report, that woman is living a fruitful life without the torment of addiction!

Whatever tough decision awaits you today, know that God is reaching out to you, saying, "I'm here for you. I want you to walk in the fullness of what I have for you. Make the righteous decision you need to make to believe and obey. You are not going to lose. You will gain more of Me."

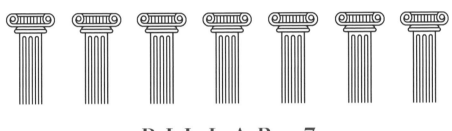

PILLAR 7

STEWARDSHIP

.

THE PROPER PERSPECTIVE

Our sons are grown men now, but Jackie and I haven't forgotten their early years. How wonderful it was to see them learn to do things themselves and hear them start to string words into short sentences. Years removed from those times, I know our fond memories are a bit incomplete. This hits me pretty much every time I take a few moments to look into our church's preschool classes.

For those two- to five-year-olds, we want them to learn three truths: God made me; God loves me; and Jesus wants to be my friend forever. But no matter how good and caring the teacher is, toddler tug-of-wars inevitably break out. Whether it's over a crayon, a chair, or a puzzle piece, when I peek in the rooms, I'll often see two determined kids grab the same thing and hold on for dear life.

"It's mine!" shouts the little boy.

"No. It's mine!" the little girl shouts back.

"Uh-uh. It's mine!"

"No. It's mine!"

At this point, if not before, the teacher intervenes and helps them figure things out. Otherwise, the standoff would never end.

Fortunately, those are the moments filtered out from my parent-memory.

We adults might smile now about the "mine-mine-mine" attitudes of toddlers, but we're not so different from them. Thanks to our sinful nature, we too like to hold onto our things. We can be selfish with our time, our money, our possessions, and even with sharing the gospel. That's why I present stewardship as the final pillar, because to be a good steward of everything God has given us, we really need the other pillars to be in place in our lives: We need godly priorities, integrity, love, loyalty, accountability, and righteousness.

> *Good stewardship starts with this proper perspective: God owns everything.*

Now please understand. I'm not saying you need to be excelling in all of those areas. You will, however, find that good stewardship becomes easier and easier as you grow in the Lord. From the beginning, God wanted us to be fruitful and to multiply what He had given us so that the Earth would be filled with healthy Christian home after healthy Christian home.

THE PROPER PERSPECTIVE: GOD OWNS IT ALL

In the dictionary, the definition of the word *steward* is this: *One who is entrusted with the property and possessions of another.* The biblical definition of a steward is: *One who uses God's resources to build God's kingdom.*

The first stewards on this planet were Adam and Eve.

> *So God created man in His own image; in the image of God He created him; male and female He created them. Then God blessed them, and God said to them, "Be fruitful and multiply; fill the earth and subdue it...."*

Genesis 1:27–28 NKJV

God's original wish for Adam and Eve was that they would take what they had in the Garden of Eden and spread it. Before their fall, Adam and Eve had the right priorities and valued God over the fruit; they saw things through God's eyes; they were loyal to God; they loved God; they were accountable to meet with Him every day. And they believed and obeyed Him. They were righteous.

But the serpent changed everything, and sin was brought into the world. Adam and Eve's priorities changed. They ran from God not to Him, and they saw things through the tempter's eyes instead of through God's. Because of this, work and gathering food became difficult, and stewardship became difficult.

Thousands of years later, stewardship is no easier, but it is still what God desires from us.

Good stewardship starts with this proper perspective: God owns everything. This fact is vital to understand, because if you feel as if you own something, you will use it selfishly. But if you know that you only steward it—that it is God's—you will use it purposefully.

We might think we own things, but we don't.

> *We brought nothing into the world, and we can take nothing out of it.*
>
> 1 Timothy 6:7 NIV

Still, this battle between ownership and stewardship is difficult. You can probably relate if you've ever started a business and poured your life into it for ten or twenty years. Even though God is telling you to "keep a loose grip on the things of this world," it can be challenging to see the business as God's. But it is.

The same goes for anyone who works for a paycheck. That money in our pockets tests us: Is it ours, or is it God's? And then God asks for our tithes—ten percent of our income. Why? To check our hearts; to force us to answer, *Do I own it, or do I steward it?* whatever "it" is.

As we look back over the story of Jacob, we can see that Jacob settled this question in his heart long before God brought him the blessing of his wives, his children, or his wealth. Jacob had the proper perspective that he was only a steward of God's resources, and he committed to honor God with a tenth of all that the Lord would provide.

> *Then Jacob made a vow, saying, "If God will be with me, and keep me in this way that I am going, and give me bread to eat and clothing to put on, so that I come back to my father's house in peace, then the Lord shall be my God. And this stone which I have set as a pillar shall be God's house, and of all that You give me I will surely give a tenth to You."*
>
> Genesis 28:20–22 NKJV

Before we can build strong lives and families, we must get the final pillar of stewardship into its proper place. We are only stewards of the blessings God has entrusted to us, and we must use the resources which flow into our hands to build God's kingdom purposefully.

FIVE THINGS WE NEED TO STEWARD WELL

Being a good steward is a high calling that requires great responsibility, but it leads to great rewards. It isn't easy, but there are several areas where we can begin to be more purposeful in how we handle the gifts which God has entrusted to us.

Here are five areas where we can start:

1. Stewarding Our Bodies

Take a deep breath now. Really. Breathe.

The breath that flowed through your lungs? It was God's—He gave it to you. Our bodies do not belong to us. We shouldn't use our bodies selfishly. They should be used purposefully.

Do you not know that your bodies are temples of the Holy Spirit, who is in you, whom you have received from God? You are not your own; you were bought at a price. Therefore honor God with your bodies.

1 Corinthians 6:19–20 NIV

A few years ago I was playing golf with my friend John Bevere. Midway through the round, I told John I was hungry and was looking forward to a cheeseburger at the turn.

"Oh, no you're not!" he replied.

My surprise and confusion must have shown on my face because he continued. "If someone gave you a Ferrari, would you just put any kind of gas in it?"

"No, I'd put the high-test in."

"Would you put recycled oil in it?" he asked.

"No, I'd put in the best oil possible."

"Well, your body is like that Ferrari." (I enjoyed that comparison.) "But, unlike a car," he continued, "you can't trade in your body. You need to take good care of it."

It was clear what he was getting at, but I couldn't resist asking, "Does this mean we're not getting cheeseburgers?"

John smiled as he reached into his bag and announced, "Here's what you're going to eat."

It was a sandwich made with Ezekiel bread (supposedly the healthiest bread in the world). Spread between the slices were almond butter and sugar-free fig jelly. That's it.

I wasn't sure I'd like John's cheeseburger alternative, but I did like the perspective he shared. "Most people eat for pleasure, not for fuel," he said. "God doesn't mind you enjoying food, but the purpose of it is to keep you strong and healthy so you can have a long-lasting influence on the world."

The Bible is clear that our bodies should be used for godly purposes, not selfish ones. Because our bodies are not our own, we should not participate in sexual immorality. Why? Sexual immorality only hurts ourselves. Every sin a person commits is outside the body, but sexual immorality has a specific toll on your flesh. Your body is the temple of the Holy Spirit. Steward it the way you're supposed to and take care of it for your own sake.

2. Stewarding Our Children and Our Relationships

Our children are not ours. We need to steward them well.

Psalm 127:3 (NKJV) says, "Behold, children are a heritage from the Lord." One translation of the word *heritage* is *property*. We are to raise our children and care for them the right way, because they're really God's children. They belong to Him. If we're going to build strong homes. We need to have the proper perspective that God has entrusted us with our children so we would raise them purposefully and guide them into His kingdom.

Whether it's with our children or anyone else in life, God asks us to steward our relationships His way. Each person represents someone whom God wants to save. If we treat people poorly, we hamper our opportunities to bring them closer to Jesus. At the same time, we should know that even when we do everything possible to share God's love with a family member, a friend, or a coworker, they may still turn away.

The thought of losing someone to the enemy is terrible, but it does bring to mind a much-repeated line from an old, black-and-white TV show I liked back in the day, *Hogan's Heroes.*

It sounds unbelievable now, but it was actually a sitcom with a World War II era prison camp as its setting. My favorite character was a guard named Sergeant Shultz. When his supervisor, Colonel Klink, would come for roll call, he would shout, "Report!"

Sgt. Shultz would respond, "All prisoners present and accounted for—Sir!"

Jesus also gave an account to His Father when He was praying in the garden of Gethsemane, just before Judas betrayed Him.

Those whom You gave Me I have kept; and none of them is lost except the son of perdition, that the Scripture might be fulfilled.

John 17:12 NKJV

All but one was present. He lost Judas, the "son of perdition." As I reflect on the one who was lost, I am actually encouraged—not because of the betrayal, but because even Jesus Himself did all He could do and still couldn't have "all present and accounted for."

Stewarding relationships is different than stewarding money. Money doesn't have a mind of its own; people do. As much as He tried, Jesus couldn't stop Judas. Go the extra mile in all your relationships, but also receive God's grace when you've done all you know to do and someone turns away.

3. Stewarding the Gospel

The Creator's command in Genesis was echoed and amplified in Jesus' Great Commission.

...Be fruitful and multiply....

Genesis 1:22 NKJV

Go therefore and make disciples of all the nations, baptizing them in the name of the Father and of the Son and of the Holy Spirit.

Matthew 28:19 NKJV

In the New Testament, there were people who were using the gospel selfishly for their own gain. But we need to use the gospel as God's stewards and share it with other people. Our spiritual gifts are not our own.

Each of you should use whatever gift you have received to serve others, as faithful stewards of God's grace in its various forms.

1 Peter 4:10 NIV

If you have the gift of prayer, the gift of teaching, or the gift of healing, don't hold it to yourself. Use it to bring people into God's kingdom!

4. Stewarding Our Earth

The earth is the Lord's, and all its fullness.

Psalm 24:1 NKJV

Being a good steward also means using the Earth purposefully.

Where I live, we felt the effects of the massive Gulf of Mexico oil spill in 2010. Countless wildlife died, and hundreds of miles of water and pristine shoreline were damaged. But we also saw through the clean-up efforts how God's creation responds and rebounds when we steward our natural resources well.

You and I can certainly contribute money to or help participate in any number of significant initiatives to keep the Earth healthy and prosperous. More typically, though, stewarding the Lord's Earth depends a lot on small acts, such as recycling.

Whether it's a massive undertaking such as cleaning up oil-soaked beaches, or a small thing such as using safer fertilizers on our lawns, they all start with this thought: I am not an owner of these resources, I am a steward. It takes effort, but caring for the Earth pleases the Lord.

5. Stewarding Our Money

Some people are surprised to learn how much the Bible says about money, wealth, and riches. With more than two thousand verses related to money and possessions, it seems clear that the Lord knew it would cause trouble for many of us. And sure enough, that danger is reflected in one of the best-known scriptures:

For the love of money is the root of all evil.

1 Timothy 6:10 KJV

Not only is this verse well known, it is often misquoted, with people dropping the *"For the love of ..."* part. Money itself is not evil. It's the *love of money*, or *the coveting of it*, that leads to no good.

What does lead to good is using money and resources for the Lord's purposes. And this is easier to do when we realize the contents in our piggy banks, billfolds, and money market accounts are the Lord's, not ours. As Haggai 2:8 tells us, the silver and gold are the Lord's.

If stewarded well, money can be used to accomplish great things for God's kingdom—great things ranging from supporting an overseas mission trip that sees people saved or hosting a neighborhood get-together that shows people how a strong Christian family lives.

When our days in this world are done, each of us will give an account to the Lord. Hebrews 9:27 says, "It is appointed for men to die once, but after this the judgment" (NKJV). Our rewards in Heaven will be determined by how we stewarded our lives, our gifts, our finances, and our opportunities. God will ask, "Did you use the resources I gave you to build My kingdom, or yours? Did you fill the Earth and multiply My kingdom, or did you keep everything I blessed you with to yourself?"

STEWARDSHIP IS MINDFUL OF THE TIME

Imagine watching a football game, and your team is behind by two touchdowns. It's the fourth quarter with only five minutes left, yet, for some reason, your team is not hustling. They're walking to the scrimmage line. They're taking their sweet time to hike the ball. Of course, if they ever hope to be victorious, they'll need to get into their hurry-up offense.

A good steward also has a sense of urgency. There is much to accomplish for the Lord, and a good steward realizes the clock is ticking. We need to make good use of our time, because our days are numbered (Psalm 90:12).

> *There is much to accomplish for the Lord, and a good steward realizes the clock is ticking.*

You have only a few years to shape your kids' lives and teach them the gospel. Are you being purposeful to fill their minds and hearts with the Word of God? One of these days, that retirement clock will sound for each of us, God willing. Are you mindful to invest and save enough money to live on, or will you be struggling to make ends meet when that day comes? Yet another sound will ring out in this world one day. The Bible describes it as a trumpet sound, signaling the return of the Lord. Are you and all your household ready to meet Him?

Now, when some people think about this, it produces fear. That's not my intention. I hope, however, that it simply emphasizes to you the importance of being mindful of how we use our time.

But what if you feel as if you've wasted your time or resources in the past? I firmly believe that if you purpose in your heart to be a better steward, God will help you.

I remember getting a note a while back from a couple, wanting to share with me how they had purposed in their hearts to get out of debt in three years. They had accumulated $21,000 of credit card debt, and they had committed themselves to stop spending selfishly and start spending purposefully. And they were successful! They paid off their credit cards, but they let me know they weren't going to stop there. They were determined to pay off their mortgage, too.

If you make that first step, God will make the next step toward you, followed by another one, and another one.

> So I will restore to you the years that the swarming locust has eaten….
>
> *Joel 2:25 NKJV*

Unfortunately, some of us have been our own locusts. But that's in the past. Determine to stop "eating" the time God has given you, and resolve to become a good steward today. **If you resolve it, God will restore it.** Believe me, God will redeem the time (Ephesians 5:16).

TAKE AN HONEST ASSESSMENT

Stewardship takes an honest look at your limitations and your giftings. You need to realize where you are, what your gifting is, and what your limitations might be. Instead of focusing on what you don't have, be a good steward of what you do have.

What has God gifted you with? Is it the ability to make money? Use it for the kingdom of God. Are you gifted to preach the gospel? Use it for the kingdom of God. Are you gifted to teach? Use it for the kingdom of God. Don't look at what you can't do; look at what you can do.

If you have trouble doing door-to-door evangelism or speaking in public, that's okay. You can share biblical truths one-on-one or lead a small group. I will say, though, that God might want to stretch you beyond what you think you can do.

In the book of Luke, Jesus tells the parable of the unjust steward whose limitations were exposed, but he was able to overcome them. The steward worked for a rich man, and one day, the master accused him of wasting the man's goods and money. He demanded an account of his stewardship.

The steward knew time was short. If he didn't do something, he was going to get fired.

> Then the steward said within himself, "What shall I do? For my master is taking the stewardship away from me. I cannot dig; I am ashamed to beg. I have resolved what to do."
>
> *Luke 16:3–4 NIV*

The steward's plan of action included visiting all the master's debtors and collecting as much money as possible. If they couldn't pay a hundred measures of oil, the steward accepted a payment of fifty. From another debtor who owed a hundred measures of grain, the steward accepted eighty. When the steward presented to the master what he had collected, the master commended the unjust steward "because he had dealt shrewdly" (Luke 16:8 NIV).

You too can make a plan of action to redeem any lost time, money, or missed opportunities. Call on God's wisdom to see what's ahead in your life:

"My kids are going to go to college...."

"I need to get out of debt...."

"I know people who need to be saved...."

"I'm going to face the Lord..."

Stewardship is not maintenance. Stewardship is multiplication.

...then ask the Lord and the people in your life for your own shrewd plan of action.

Every barrier that limits you can be overcome through the solution of good stewardship.

SEIZE YOUR OPPORTUNITIES AND SECURE THE FUTURE

God wants us to secure the future—not just for ourselves but for the lost and for the next generation. God wants His kingdom to be filled. When you're caring for the lost, you're building God's kingdom. When you're taking care of the generation who are coming after you, raising them up in the nurture and admonition of the Lord, that's being a good steward.

Stewardship is about securing the future. It's not just about holding on to the present.

My friend John Bevere also shared this wise, biblical insight with me: **"Stewardship is not maintenance. Stewardship is multiplication."**

The idea comes from Jesus' parable of the talents. The story, which is told in the books of Matthew and Luke, begins with a man giving his servants "talents" (gold) before the master goes on a trip. One servant got five talents, another got two talents, and the third servant got one talent.

The man who had received five bags of gold went at once and put his money to work. He gained five bags more. So also, the one with two bags of gold gained two more. But the man who had received one bag went off, became fearful, dug a hole in the ground, and hid his master's money.

> *Then the man who had received one bag of gold came. "Master,"*
> *he said, "I knew that you are a hard man, harvesting where you*
> *have not sown and gathering where you have not scattered seed.*
> *So I was afraid and went out and hid your gold in the ground. See,*
> *here is what belongs to you."*
>
> *His master replied, "You wicked, lazy servant! So you knew that*
> *I harvest where I have not sown and gather where I have not*
> *scattered seed? Well then, you should have put my money on*
> *deposit with the bankers, so that when I returned I would have*
> *received it back with interest."*
>
> *Matthew 25:24–27 NIV*

The man thought he was doing the right thing by not losing the one talent, but that's wrong thinking! Stewardship is multiplication.

God is going to give you opportunities to multiply what He has given you. Seize those opportunities to use your life and the gospel to win souls. Use your money to feed the poor. Use your knowledge of the Word to teach a teenager. Ask the Lord for creative ideas to prosper and advance His kingdom, and He will give them to you.

That's how Jacob prospered. God gave him a plan in a dream that seemed ridiculous in the natural, but in the end, Jacob worked his plan with intense focus and walked away with an incredible fortune of every black, speckled, and striped sheep and goat from Laban's flocks.

> *And it came to pass, whenever the stronger livestock conceived, that*
> *Jacob placed the rods before the eyes of the livestock in the gutters,*
> *that they might conceive among the rods. But when the flocks were*
> *feeble, he did not put them in; so the feebler were Laban's and*
> *the stronger Jacob's. Thus the man became exceedingly prosperous,*
> *and had large flocks, female and male servants, and camels and*
> *donkeys.*
>
> *Genesis 30:41–43 NKJV*

God gives us great opportunities to do all He has called us to do. I encourage you to look at your home, your relationships, your bank account, and your calendar, and strike the word "mine" from your vocabulary. Seek ways to be fruitful and to multiply His gifts. Be a wise steward who uses God's resources to build God's kingdom.

Let God use your life, your money, and your talents to fill the Earth with His glory. **Build His kingdom with the pillar of stewardship, and God will build your house and make it strong.**

BUILDING STRONG

I love how God's perfect Word doesn't present a perfect world. The people we read about in the Bible lived thousands of years ago, but they were just as flawed as we are today. Their circumstances and situations weren't always like the things we face today, but like us, in good times and bad, they had a choice: *Do I live for God, or do I live for myself?*

Jacob was far from perfect, but he loved God. He listened for God's will and tried to follow it.

Practically from birth, Jacob lived under a shadow. Not only did his name reflect a negative characteristic, "heel-grabber," it likely was a constant reminder to him and others that he entered this world in "second place." That label wasn't fair, but it was Jacob's reality. His culture elevated firstborns—people who came first in life.

Oh, how wonderful for Jacob, and for you and me, that God's ways aren't the world's ways.

Despite Jacob's reputation, despite the sins and mistakes he made, God used him. Jacob endured much in his life, from having to work for his father-in-law for twenty years in his younger years, to later seeing his family suffer through a drought and being racked by grief, thinking his son Joseph had been killed.

Through it all, Jacob followed God in the best way he could.

When Jacob wrestled God and wouldn't let go until he was blessed, Jacob was given a new name—*Israel*. In Hebrew, the name literally combined the words for *wrestle* and *God*. It is often translated as "Prince of God."

Prince. The person first in line behind the king. Yes, the King of the Universe, Almighty God, declared Jacob a first finisher. The Lord tells Jacob and us, "It doesn't matter how the world sees you. It's how I see you that matters."

God declared Jacob a victor because Jacob valued God's priorities and took responsibility for his household. He swore to his own hurt and worked with integrity and loyalty for Laban for twenty years. He loved his family and God with all his might and made himself accountable, allowing God to deliver him of his insecurities. Jacob walked in righteousness, believing and obeying God's instructions, and he stewarded all the blessings he had received.

Then, perhaps so that Jacob would always remember the place where he was freed of his insecurities, he was given a limp—a small price to pay for the healing that came. Jacob limped the rest of his life, but not on the inside. In his heart he knew, "I am first with God."

We are all living with our own kinds of limps and hurts, reminders that situations in life—some we created ourselves, some brought about by others—can harm us. We can let them defeat us, or we can learn from them and gain victory.

I pray that as we have studied the life of Jacob together, you have truly embraced the seven key pillars that are woven throughout his life and the Scripture to help you build a strong and overcoming life through Christ Jesus.

These seven principles are easy to commit to memory:

PRIORITIES
INTEGRITY
LOYALTY
LOVE
ACCOUNTABILITY
RIGHTEOUSNESS
STEWARDSHIP

They are the "finish first" essentials we need to put into practice for ourselves, for our families, for our careers, and for God's kingdom.

Let me remind you of the words of Paul which apply to us all:

I can do all things through Christ who strengthens me.

Philippians 4:13 NKJV

In Christ, you can build a strong life. You can finish first in life, love, and work.

Friend, I pray that you will build into your family and home the seven pillars of a strong and healthy walk with God. I pray that you will seek His wisdom and make it the foundation for every decision you make.

Build strong, and finish first!

A PRAYER OF SALVATION

Friend,

If you have never prayed a prayer to ask Jesus Christ to become your Lord and Savior, today can be your day of salvation!

Jesus Christ is God the Son, the second person of the Trinity. Jesus came to Earth, lived a sinless life, performed miracles, and died on the cross for mankind to purchase our redemption from sin. We are saved by grace through faith in Jesus Christ and His death, burial, and resurrection. Salvation is a gift from God. It isn't a result of our good works or any human efforts.

To put your trust in what Jesus accomplished for you, pray this prayer, and accept His gift of salvation today:

Dear God,

I know I'm a sinner, and I ask for Your forgiveness. I believe Jesus Christ is Your Son. I believe that He died for my sin and that You raised Him to life. I want to trust Him as my Savior and follow Him as my Lord from this day forward. Guide my life and help me to do Your will.

I pray this in the name of Jesus. Amen.

If you prayed that prayer to make Jesus Christ your Lord and Savior, please let us know at *destinyworshipcenter.com* so that we can help you take your next steps in becoming a fully devoted follower of Christ.

RECOMMENDED RESOURCES

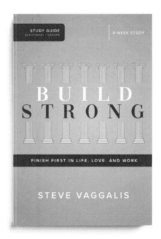

BUILD STRONG: DEVOTIONAL
AND SMALL GROUP STUDY GUIDE

The reason most people get frustrated in life is because they don't understand God's plan. The *BUILD STRONG: Devotional and Small Group Study Guide* is a personal devotional guide you can use right in your own home, and the bonus small group discussion material can be used in any church, family, or group of friends wanting to dive deeper into these concepts. The devotional guide is designed for people of every age and stage of their walk with Christ and provides a wonderful way to take what you've learned in this book and start applying it immediately.

As you work through the personal devotional lessons each day, you'll be equipped and encouraged to build a strong life on the foundation of wisdom, while incorporating each of the seven pillars of success. As you learn more and begin to practice the life-application principles, you'll grow stronger in your relationships with God and your loved ones, and you'll enjoy the journey along the way!

Start building strong and learn how to finish first in life, love, and work. Visit *destinyworshipcenter.com/buildstrong* to get your companion guide and/or small group kit today.

ABOUT THE AUTHOR

Marked by knowledge and honor, Pastor Steve Vaggalis delivers a book with the core foundations and pillars of his life and family. Steve holds a bachelor's degree in theology from Liberty Bible College and has served in ministry for more than three decades. In 2001, Steve and his wife, Jackie, founded Destiny Worship Center, located in Destin, Florida. Through Steve's dynamic leadership this interdenominational church has grown from one hundred people in attendance at their first meeting, to thousands of people throughout multiple regional campuses.

Pastor Steve and Jackie are beyond blessed to have their eldest son, Steven, and his wife, Tiffany, as well as their youngest son, Victor, and his wife, Samantha, serve with them in ministry. Together as a family, they enjoy family time, golf, and travel.

NOTES

—WISDOM—

NOTES

—PRIORITIES—

NOTES

—INTEGRITY—

NOTES

—LOYALTY—

NOTES

—LOVE—

NOTES

—ACCOUNTABILITY—

NOTES

—RIGHTEOUSNESS—

NOTES

—STEWARDSHIP—